# Glyn Trefor-Jones

Glyn Trefor-Jones is a theatre director, writer and teacher. Having gained a degree in Modern History and Politics from Cardiff University, he went on to pursue his creative ambitions by studying Acting and Musical Theatre at Hertfordshire Theatre School and, later, acting and creative writing at AARTS International.

Having toured extensively as an actor, performing in a variety of theatre, corporate and television work, he began to write and tour his own work, establishing Prospero Productions, Liberty Productions and the Bedford Rep Theatre Company. He has written extensively for young people as well as writing, directing and producing his own musicals under the production company Glyn Trefor-Jones Presents. His latest work, *Sunsets and Mornings* (book and lyrics by Glyn Trefor-Jones, music by David Jonathan), recently premiered at the Castle Theatre, Wellingborough.

He has always combined his theatre engagements with teaching work and has worked for an eclectic array of drama schools, youth theatre companies, schools and drama groups in both the UK and USA.

In 2005, Glyn established The Academy of Performing Arts, a part-time theatre school for young people between the ages of five and seventeen. The Academy quickly flourished into a thriving training academy with centres across Bedfordshire and Warwickshire. Glyn remains the creative director of all schools and continues to teach acting and musical theatre.

His first book, *Drama Menu: Theatre Games in Three Courses*, was published by Nick Hern Books in 2015 and has become a bestseller for drama teachers and workshop leaders around the world.

Glyn Trefor-Jones

## AT A DISTANCE
### 80 Socially Distanced or Online Theatre Games

NICK HERN BOOKS
London
www.nickhernbooks.co.uk

*Drama Menu at a Distance*
first published in Great Britain in 2020
by Nick Hern Books Limited,
The Glasshouse, 49a Goldhawk Road, London W12 8QP

Designed and typeset by Nick Hern Books, London
Printed and bound in Great Britain by
Mimeo Ltd, Huntingdon, Cambridgeshire PE29 6XX

A CIP catalogue record for this book
is available from the British Library

ISBN 978 1 84842 979 6

Woodland
CARBON
www.woodlandcarbon.co.uk
NICK HERN BOOKS
Printed on Carbon Captured paper

# Contents

# Introduction

Welcome to this special edition of *Drama Menu* – and, this time, it's all about working at a safe distance.

Since the COVID-19 pandemic began spreading across the world in 2020, we have faced challenges like never before. For those of us who teach and lead drama classes and workshops, it must be our priority to do so in a safe, secure, healthy way – whilst also observing social distancing, in order to protect our students and halt the spread of the disease. But, as the old adage goes... the show must go on! At a time when performers are needed more than ever, training the next generation of performers must also go on!

This book contains eighty games and exercises that offer fun, creative, learning experiences without the need to get up close and personal. Several exercises have been adapted from *Drama Menu* due to their appropriateness for socially distanced play, whilst the rest are new exercises that have been devised with distance in mind. Even at a distance, drama training can still be vibrant, engaging, energising and extremely rewarding – and these exercises set out to increase every player's performance abilities as well as respecting the rules of social distancing.

So... is what follows simply eighty different ways of performing a monologue? Fortunately not! In fact, a great many of these exercises require lots of creative cooperation, collaboration and connection so, with some creative thinking, even without entering into the personal space of others, a collective learning experience can be achieved.

For however long we must keep our distance, we will continue to create, to reinvent, to strive and to feed our creativity. Performers are resilient and resourceful and we won't let a little thing like distance come between us and the drama! I invite you to embrace the new normal (for now) and I very much hope that you enjoy the book, and find it useful with your students, participants and players, in whatever setting you work.

# The Menu

For those of you familiar with the *Drama Menu* concept, you'll find that the format of this book remains the same. The eighty exercises are categorised into menu-inspired 'courses' that increase in difficulty (and dramatic potential) as you progress through the book. Even at a distance, you will find the same progressive approach to theatre training, with exercises categorised into ever-more engaging courses. Just like a menu in a restaurant, you should choose one exercise from each course (or two if you're feeling hungry) until you have a satisfying feast ready to be consumed!

The courses are laid out as follows:

## Appetisers

These fast-paced warm-up exercises are devised to engage and enthuse, and are subdivided into 'Circle' and 'Non-Circle' Appetisers. Circle games can be a very effective tool for maintaining distance, but it's important to ensure that you have a large enough space in order to form an appropriately socially distanced circle.

## Starters

With Appetisers consumed, the players will be energised, engaged and after something more challenging to satisfy their dramatic appetite. The Starters are the intermediary courses providing just that challenge – and then some! Players should be creatively stretched in this course and prepared for the final challenges to come...

## Main Courses

The pinnacle of any meal, the Main Course provides the biggest test and also packs the largest creative punch. This is the time for practitioners to step back and allow the players to step up and do what they do best: devise, create and perform! All Main Courses in this book conclude with a performance piece.

## Desserts

In this book, the Dessert course is devoted to games that work best in an online setting. So, if you haven't yet returned to leading drama sessions with participants physically present, then these games will 'zoom' you through this difficult period until we can all meet again, in person, in the playing area! You will also find most of the Desserts can be played in person as well – though make sure players keep socially distanced at all times, of course.

Throughout the book there are also a great many exercises which are particularly useful as they can be employed in a physical setting *and*, with a bit of adaptation and ingenuity, in a virtual/digital workshop as well. These are indicated with the following symbol: 💻

There is also a comprehensive Resource Pack available to download as an A4 PDF, which contains all the resources required to get the very best out of each exercise. If there is a script/worksheet/printout needed it is indicated at the top of the page, just above the game number, with the following: ★. Visit www.nickhernbooks.co.uk/drama-menu-at-a-distance and download the Resource Pack. Find the desired resource and print out the required number of copies (ensuring that you have one copy per student to avoid sharing of resources), and make it even easier to unlock the true potential of the book and quickly deliver engaging and inspiring drama sessions.

All in all, *Drama Menu at a Distance* serves up a theatre training in four courses which is not diluted by the lack of physical connection. The exercises in this book have been specially selected to nourish the creativity of all participants; even without getting up close and personal, players will find that they are still able to give of themselves, to share and connect with their fellow performers, and to enjoy a creatively fulfilling and progressive experience.

# Staying Safe

The safety of the players in your group must be of paramount importance. Drama at a distance can provide as creative and rewarding a learning experience as an unrestricted session, but you must always keep one eye on the safety aspect of the work to ensure that it is fun-filled and engaging whilst also adhering to social distancing. Here are some suggestions on how to achieve this:

## Choose an appropriately sized space

Use as large a space as you have available. The more room that you have to work in, the easier it will be for players to keep a social distance.

## Pace your session appropriately

It is important to work at a pace that allows players to adhere to social-distancing rules. Too much running around excitedly will quickly lead to a breakdown of distancing discipline!

## Utilise all available spaces

Where possible, send players away to rehearse in other spaces (or even outside) to ensure that they are able to work without encroaching into the space of others. You should continually monitor the learning and always insist that work is done at a safe distance.

## Restrict the use of props

The sharing of props should be avoided. Where an exercise requires the use of a phone, ask that players use their own, ensuring that it is turned off.

## Position the audience appropriately

When showing and presenting performance pieces, place the audience in the round wherever possible. This will help to maintain maximum distance between players and audience members.

## Use furniture to reinforce distancing

Using well-placed furniture in the playing area is a great way of maintaining a safe distance. If you ask for three players to enter the playing area, they are extremely likely to gather close together – but, if you place three appropriately spaced chairs in the playing area and ask them to sit, then they will, without having being asked to do so, distance themselves suitably from their fellow players.

## Be considerate

Spatial awareness is an important attribute for any performer – and now is very much the time for them to display it! Encourage all players to make full use of their spatial-awareness skills to remain distanced from both their fellow performers and the audience, in order to keep everyone safe. At the time of writing, face coverings are not required to be worn within classrooms in UK schools, provided that social distancing is followed. If this guidance changes (or teachers feel more comfortable with the use of face coverings), then most exercises in this book will work equally well, but players should be encouraged to use maximum diction in order to make themselves clearly heard.

## Be clean

Good hygiene is (even more) essential at all times. Participants should be required to sanitise their hands before and after every session, and before and after any contact with objects or props. All chairs/props/equipment should also be thoroughly sanitised before use and, similarly, cleaned at the end of each session. If paper scripts, slips, resources or worksheets are used, you should ensure that there is a copy for each player to avoid the need for sharing, and they should be put in the recycling bin after the session (or taken home by the player). Alternatively, consider using laminated worksheets and scripts, but these should be sanitised and stored safely for reuse.

## Be respectful

This is the most important aspect of all. Performers should always be respectful of one another and understand that keeping a safe distance is for the good of everyone, both those inside and outside of the room.

# Staying Safe Online

The welfare of your group must also be paramount if you are working online in a digital space. The following guidance explains how to keep players safe in the virtual classroom, and is specifically written for those using Zoom as your platform of choice (other platforms may feature slightly different features). You should consider all these guidelines whichever platform you're using, and make sure you know how the technology works before you begin doing so with young people.

## Get parental permission

If you are working with young people or vulnerable adults online, you should always ask a parent/guardian to email their written permission before accepting them into the session. If you intend to record the session, you should seek written permission for this too.

## Lock the classroom

If your class has started and all your pupils have arrived, be sure to lock your virtual classroom to ensure that no one can crash the theatrical party.

## Use virtual waiting rooms

This feature allows you to hold potential participants in a separate 'waiting room', so you can check who they are before allowing them entry. There's also a setting to allow known students to skip the waiting room, so you don't have to manually allow thirty participants in every time.

## Disable private messaging

By disabling private messaging between players, you can prevent them from talking to one another without your knowledge and keep their focus on the session.

## Enable two-factor authentication

Generate a random meeting ID when scheduling your event and always require a password to join the meeting.

## Mute participants

As the session host, you can block unwanted, distracting or inappropriate noise from participants by muting them (if only it were that easy in an 'actual' classroom!). It's often a good idea to mute everyone when they join the session (by enabling 'mute upon entry' in your settings) and encourage players to use the 'raise hand' option if they want to speak.

## Disable file transfer

In-meeting file transfer allows people to share files through the chat. Turn this off to keep the chat from getting bombarded with unsolicited content.

## Control screen-sharing

To maintain control over what participants are seeing and to prevent anyone else from displaying unsolicited content, ensure that screen-sharing is switched to 'Only Host'.

## Set a dress code

Before the session, ask that all players are appropriately dressed when logging in... They may think that it's okay to rock up in their pyjamas, but you should make it known that it is very much not!

## Find a suitable space

The bedroom is *not* a suitable learning space – and this should be established with no ifs, buts or maybes! Players should find a suitable space in their home that allows them the freedom to move and fully express themselves.

## Establish expectations

Players should be made aware that, although the session is being hosted via a different medium, the expectations are exactly the same as if it were a physical class. Players are expected to listen, give their all, respect one another, and offer full support to their peers.

# Appetisers

This fun-filled first course provides a wide selection of warm-up activities to enthuse and energise the group before moving on to more expansive work. The Appetisers are divided into Circle Appetisers and Non-Circle Appetisers. Mix and match these Appetisers as required until the players are fully warmed up and ready to move on.

# Circle Appetisers

Circle games provide the perfect platform for social distancing. By having players stand two metres apart in a large a circle, it is easy to achieve, maintain and monitor distancing without affecting the enjoyment or outcome of the exercise.

The size of the created circle should reflect the number of players within the group, so a particularly large group will require a correspondingly large space. If you find that your space is a little too snug to fit everyone into one circle, then divide the players into two groups and have them play one group at a time; this solution works perfectly well as Circle Appetisers are generally quick-fire affairs, and players won't be waiting around for too long before it's their turn.

# 1

# Mime Story Circle

An inclusive exercise that uses mime to create a cohesive and progressive narrative.

Ask the players to stand in a socially distanced circle, and explain that you're all going to combine your creative resources to tell a story. But this will be no ordinary story... oh no! This will be a story told without words; the only medium used to convey the tale will be actions and sounds.

With this exercise, it's best to keep the explanations to a minimum and just dive straight in (the players will soon get the idea) – so, without further ado, announce that you will start the story, at which point you should move to the centre of the circle and perform an action and sound combination... Let's say, you make a strong digging action accompanied by a deep grunt before returning to your place in the circle. This is the starting point of the story and with the first element in place, it's time to build the narrative.

Ask the player to your right to add the next element to the story by entering the circle, repeating your digging and grunting combination, and then performing their own action and sound combination... Now, here's the important bit: the action and sound that they create must connect to yours and must progress the story, so they may dig and grunt before pointing at the created hole and gasping in amazement! Now, invite the next player in the circle to dig, grunt, point, gasp and then add their own combination. This continues until the story has come to a natural end or the narrative has lost its way.

Acceptance is key here. Insist that players accept the ideas of others and offer their own creative input. This cycle of offering and accepting will ensure that the mimed story maintains a clear direction.

Once the first storyline has played out, have a discussion about the skills required to make the mimed story work: awareness, acceptance, listening, clarity, focus... it's amazing how many skills are highlighted in this simple exercise. Then, with these all-important skills at the forefront of their minds, start a brand-new Mime Story and continue the process of stopping and restarting until all players have had their opportunity to contribute.

This exercise works excellently at a distance because the players are able to work creatively with their fellow performers, sharing ideas to build a narrative.

# Heads Up, Heads Down

**The game promotes concentration, group awareness and is excellent for bringing focus to the start of the session.**

Ask the players to stand in a socially distanced circle. If there is an even number of players, you get to play (yay!). But, if there is an odd number, you must step outside the circle (boo!).

The rules are simple: when you call out 'Heads down!', all players must look – guess where? That's right – down to the floor! Whilst looking down, they should decide (in their heads) who they are going to look at when they hear the call of 'Heads up!' The aim is not to be looking at someone who is also looking back at them. Focus should be sent out to the group here, as players attempt to tune into the others around them before deciding who they believe will *not* return their gaze! Now, call out 'Heads up!', accompanied by a clap to increase the urgency.

If two players are looking at one another, once eye contact is made, they must crumple to the ground (in mock agony) and they are both out of the game! This continues until only one person is left standing, and they are declared the winner!

From my experience, some players will tend to rely on the 'dark arts' to ensure that they progress to the latter stages of the game, so here are some 'misdemeanours' to look out for and ward against:

★ On the call of 'Heads up!', players must look directly towards another player who is 'in play'. Looking at the floor/ceiling/thin air is not in the spirit of the game.

★ Players must not look up, see a pair of eyes staring at them and quickly avert their gaze.

★ Looking at the same person consecutively or continuously is forbidden.

You will need eyes in the back of your head but, when played correctly, it's an excellent game for encouraging focus, concentration and connection between players.

# 3

# 5-Second Rule

Focus, concentration and remaining cool under pressure are key skills in this quick-fire circle game.

Ask the players to stand in a socially distanced circle and explain that each player will, in turn, be given a subject and they have five seconds to name three items/objects/people from that given subject in order to remain in the game...

You should stand in the centre of the circle and announce the first subject – let's say 'Winter Clothing' – whilst pointing towards your first 'victim'. As you point, you should hold up your non-pointing hand (palm outwards) and use your retracting fingers to visually display the five-second countdown. If the player names three items of winter clothing within the five seconds, they remain standing. If not, they sit down.

Now, move on to the next player and announce a new subject. Examples of possible subjects might be:

★ Things you'd find in a fridge.
★ Famous novels.
★ Pop songs.
★ School subjects.
★ Animals you'd find in a zoo.
★ Movies
★ Things starting with 'B'.
★ Holiday destinations.
★ Ways to become a millionaire.

Continue playing until you have navigated the whole circle and are back at the start. It's time now to ramp up the pressure, so navigate the circle again, only this time the standing players must name *four* things from their given subject. If there are still players standing after this, go for five, six, seven... until you're left with only one player: the winner!

This is a particularly versatile game, as you can tailor the subjects to suit the age of your group. With younger players, go with a subject like Disney films, and with older participants maybe plays by Shakespeare... Not only is it fun, but it can also be very educational!

# Someone Else's Number

**4**

An inclusive concentration exercise that improves focus and concentration.

Ask the group to stand in a socially distanced circle and, starting with yourself, number the players in turn in a clockwise direction from one. Choose one member of the group to start off, and explain that the only rule is that they have to say someone else's number. Once they have said someone else's number (e.g. 'Five'), Player 5 must say someone else's number... This continues until there is a cannon of people saying someone else's number in succession! Once everyone has got the hang of it, pause the game and explain that, if a player pauses or hesitates before saying someone else's number, then they are out.

Restart the game and, once someone pauses or hesitates, declare them to be 'out' and ask them to sit down. That number is now out of commission and from now on, if someone pauses or hesitates, they are out... but if they say a number that is out of commission, they are also out. Continue this until you get down to the last two players, who can be joint winners.

This is a really useful exercise for enthusing and focusing the group at the beginning of a session. For some reason, many groups like to stand on chairs for this exercise (and sit on them once they are out). Not sure why this is, but I would recommend that you try – with appropriately sturdy chairs and appropriately mature participants!

# 5

# Apple-Apple-Apple

**An effective concentration game for smaller groups.**

Ask the group to stand in a socially distanced circle and, once assembled, explain that each player is going to be assigned their very own fruit name. It's important for players to pay attention at this stage as they will need to remember not only their own fruit, but also the full array of fruits available. As you navigate the circle assigning fruits, try to go for fruits with short-ish names – apple, pear, kiwi, lime, etc.... the reason for this will soon become clear.

Once all fruit names have been allocated, stand in the middle of the circle and explain that, sadly, you are without a fruit and that, the only way for you to get one is by saying the name of someone else's fruit *three times* before that person can say it *once*. So, you might say 'Apple–apple–apple' (at three million miles an hour) in the hope that the player who has been allocated the 'apple' is not focused and doesn't say 'apple' once. If you manage to catch the apple out then you become the apple, and the deposed apple must enter the circle having lost their fruit name. He/she must then attempt to regain fruit status by saying the name of a fruit three times... You should ensure that adequate diction is used in the fruity delivery – 'Banana–nana–nana' does not count as three bananas!

The object of the exercise is to remain switched-on and fully focused, so that the players protect their fruit status, and keep the fruitless player in the middle of the circle for as long as possible. It's amazing how quickly minds can wander so, after a few failed attempts, encourage the players to have two minutes of total fruity-focus and fully commit to the task at hand. They will find that, by remaining fully focused and concentrated, the game will be completely transformed and it will be much more difficult to steal another player's fruit.

It is important for players to draw on these high levels of intensity and focus; bringing such a skill-set to the playing area will always transform the work and make for a much more dynamic experience. Players working at an intense level will connect more deeply with their fellow performers and, when this is applied to performance, the watching audience will be drawn in by their focus, passion and intensity. What started as a ridiculous, fruit-based game will have highlighted a vital set of skills that players should take with them into their future work.

# Wink Murder

A classic game that younger players universally love, and which promotes concentration, group awareness and is also lots of fun.

Ask the group to sit in a socially distanced circle and choose one member of the group to become a 'detective'. The detective must now stand outside the room (or turn their back on the group) whilst you choose a 'murderer' from the circle. Choose your murderer by pointing (silently) at one participant and ensuring that all others (apart from the detective) are aware of who the dastardly villain is... It is a good idea with very young players to ask if anyone can't wink before choosing the murderer, as this will save having an extremely long and uneventful game! Once the murderer has been chosen, invite the detective back into the circle – I usually do this by song...

All chant 'Detective, detective, there's going to be a murder', followed by a *Pink Panther*-inspired 'Di-dum, di-dum, di-dum di-dum di-dum di-dum di-duuuuum, dum-a-di-dum!' If that means nothing to you then it might be a good idea to make up your own chant!

Once the detective is standing in the middle of the circle, the murdering can begin! The chosen murderer dispatches his/her victims by winking at them. When the victim receives their fatal wink, they must perish in a predetermined style of death (over-the-top, operatic, French... the variations are endless). Once they have uttered their final words, the victims must lie back to signify that they are out of the game.

The aim of the game is for the detective to discover the murderer before all players meet a grizzly end. Detectives are permitted three guesses to discover the identity of the murderer. Once the murderer has been discovered (or the three guesses are up), count up the fatalities and start a new game, encouraging the next murderer to up the crime rate.

# 7

# Hands in the Bushes

**This fun group-energiser improves listening, concentration and coordination skills.**

Ask the group to sit in a large, socially distanced circle and, once everyone is sitting comfortably (including you), thrust both hands in front of your body and, with a showbiz, jazz-hand motion, call out: 'Hands in the bushes!'

The players will be a little bewildered by this outburst, but ignore the puzzled gazes and quickly encourage them to join in with you and to call out in unison, 'Hands in the bushes!' – not forgetting the jazz-hand motion. Once this opening call-to-arms has been made, start to clap out a rhythm by striking your knees with both hands twice and then clapping hands together twice. Once again, encourage the players to join in.

When you have a good rhythm going (not too fast... yet!), it's time to pick a subject and get the game underway. Maintaining the clapping rhythm throughout, call out: 'Give me...' (two beats) 'Names of...' (two beats) 'Countries...' (two beats) 'To my left...' (two beats) 'Starting with...' (two beats) 'Austria...' (two beats)...

Now we know that the subject is 'Countries' and that the direction of travel is to the left so, continuing the rhythm, the player to your left must allow two beats/claps before calling out a different country – 'Iceland...' (two beats) – then the player to their left calls out another – 'Germany...' (two beats) – and so it goes on around the circle until someone repeats a country, speaks out of rhythm or doesn't say anything at all. When this happens, stop the exercise, choose a player to pick a new subject and start over with the jazz hands and 'Hands in the bushes!'

The idea of the exercise is to get all the way around the circle without any repetition or speaking out of rhythm. This can only be achieved by teamwork, listening and concentration, which makes it a very effective group warm-up.

# What Are You Doing?

**An inclusive and energetic exercise that encourages forward-thinking, creativity and improves mime skills.**

Ask the group to stand in a socially distanced circle (of which you will become a part). Once created, you should step into the circle and perform a simple mime, such as flying a kite. As you struggle to control your wayward kite in the strong breeze, you should instruct the player who was next to you in the circle to ask 'What are you doing?' and when asked, you must respond with something other than 'flying a kite'... Let's go with 'scrubbing the floor'.

This response will cause great confusion (and maybe a little derision) from the group, but explain that, when you return to your place in the circle, the person who asked 'What are you doing?' must enter the circle and perform what you'd said you were doing – i.e. the mime of scrubbing the floor. When the floor-scrubber is asked 'What are you doing?' by the next player in the circle, they will reply with an altogether different activity... 'Walking a tightrope', which the incoming player must then mime. This continues until everyone has performed a mime and made an offer.

Once they've got the idea, encourage the group to think of increasingly challenging, contrasting and energised activities that will really put the miming abilities of the players to the test, before restarting the exercise at double speed! This extra dimension demands that players think fast, throw themselves into every activity with gusto, and by the end of the round, there will be a tangible buzz of excitement in the room.

# 9

# 1-Word Story

**This creative exercise encourages listening, creativity and teamwork.**

Ask the group (including you) to sit in a socially distanced circle. Once you are all sitting comfortably, inform the players that they are about to devise a brand-new, never-before-heard story. And what does every good story begin with? You got it: 'Once upon a time…'

So, begin the exercise by saying the word 'Once', before encouraging the person next to you to say the word 'upon'; the next to say 'a'; and the next, 'time'! After these time-honoured words have been uttered, the players are free to create at will, so continue going around the circle saying one word each until a new story has been told.

After a couple of practice runs, it's a good idea to set a title for your story before restarting, which helps to focus the work and prevent the created stories from becoming too silly! Here are some ideas:

★ *The Genie's Three Wishes*
★ *The Curse of the Angry Witch*
★ *Michael's Magic Potion*

## Variation: 1-Word Story Pairs

Once the players have got the concept, place two chairs (not too close, and facing opposite directions) in the playing area and invite two players to sit. Once seated, set a title for a story and give them thirty seconds to amuse and enthral the class with a weird and wonderful tale, written one word at a time, alternating between them.

Have a discussion with the group at the end about how interesting the story was and how well the players worked together. Were they listening to one another? Did the story make sense? Were we entertained? With discussion over, invite two new players into the playing area, set a new title and… restart the storytelling!

Appetisers

# Alan Sells Apples in Albania

> A quick-fire exercise that improves group concentration and encourages performers to remain calm and focused under pressure.

Ask the players to stand in a socially distanced circle and, once created, place yourself in the centre of that circle. The game begins when you point at a player in the circle and call out a letter at random. They now have to think fast and say the following, all beginning with the chosen letter:

1. A person's *name*.

2. *What* they sell.

3. The country *where* they sell it.

So 'A' could lead to 'Alan sells Apples in Albania'. 'B' might be 'Bertie sells Balloons in Botswana'. 'C' could be... well, I think you get the concept!

Once pointed at, players must think fast and give their answers immediately; if they pause, hesitate or make up a name, product or country that doesn't exist, they are out and must sit down; if they succeed, they remain standing. Continue going around the circle, giving a different letter to each participant until only one player remains. They're the winner.

Discourage players from calling out answers to help struggling contestants. Although it's admirable that they're attempting to help their fellow (flailing) performer, in the theatre, audience members don't call out our lines if we forget them. In order to prepare for that eventuality, players should be very much on their own when they come face to face with a pointed finger and a letter of the alphabet!

Remaining calm under pressure is key here. If players tense up and place themselves under too much pressure, it will be much more difficult to achieve the task at hand. By remaining calm, focused and relaxed, they will find that they are more able to declare with confidence and conviction that Denise does indeed sell Diamonds in Denmark!

Appetisers

# Non-Circle Appetisers

Once the players have devoured a Circle Appetiser (or two), it's time to break free from the circle and play some Non-Circle Appetisers.

These games usually require a good deal of travelling and physical interaction with the other players, but here all travelling has been curtailed and the contact cut out – but the physical and focused nature of the games is retained.

# Machines

**A physical warm-up that visually demonstrates the importance of working as a cohesive company.**

Ask the group to form an audience around the perimeter of the room and mark out six 'Action Areas' in the playing area, like this:

| 1 | 2 | 3 |
|---|---|---|
| 6 | 5 | 4 |

Now instruct a player sitting near Action Area 1 to enter the playing area and to perform a repetitious movement and sound. This might be a karate-chop motion with a 'Whoosh' sound, a jumping motion with a 'Boing', or perhaps a punch of the air with a 'Wahoo' – you get the idea; it should be something physically and vocally dynamic!

Once Player 1 is in full flow, it's time to build the machine! Ask Player 1 to repeat their action and sound continually, before inviting a player near Action Area 2 to enter the playing area and become the second moving part of the machine, by positioning themselves in the space and performing their own repetitive action and sound. Continue until all six areas are occupied with players performing actions and sounds – and one huge machine has been created.

After the first attempt, invariably the machine will not be a cohesive collaboration of moving parts, seamlessly working as one, but is more likely to be a collection of individuals doing their own thing. Stop the exercise and explain that the power of theatre comes from a company of players working in unison towards a common goal, not a group of individuals showing off! The machine's movements and sounds should be interlinked, each one driven by and affecting the others, so players should consider carefully before creating their machine part. After a couple of attempts, this message should be visually reinforced by the creation of a much more cohesive and connected machine. I like to end this particular exercise by speeding up the machine until it explodes – although this may not be appropriate with all groups!

*Note: If you're playing online, speed the machine up by raising one hand and blow it up by raising two!*

# Slow-Motion Race

> This exercise encourages physical connection and control, and a strong sense of spatial awareness.

Ask the players to stand in a straight line and explain that they're going to have a race. If there are too many players to stand in a socially distanced line then you will need to run more than one race. Once the players are lined up and ready to go, declare the finish line to be... about three paces from the start! It's a good idea to mark the finish line with string/tape/chairs ... whatever you have at your disposal so that the goal is clear. The 'athletes' will be somewhat bemused by this ridiculously short running track, but explain that this is no ordinary race; this will be a slow-motion race, with the winner being the *last* player to cross the line.

Continue to explain that players must *look* like they are racing as fast as they can at all times or they will be disqualified. They must keep moving forwards at all times or they will also be disqualified – some players will try to tread water or even 'run' backwards, so be vigilant and disqualify those non-movers! Once players have been disqualified or once they have crossed the line, they must immediately revert to 'fast motion' and run clear of the finish line (this will afford you a better view of the players still in the race).

So are you ready...? Are you set...? Well, not quite! To add an extra element of drama to the racing, it's a good idea to strike up the *Chariots of Fire* theme on the sound system. This emotive music will provide the perfect backdrop to your slow-motion race! Now, you're all set so, call out: 'On your marks... Get set... GO!'

On the call of 'GO!', you will be greeted by the most bizarre sight of sinews tensing, sweat pouring, but very little forward movement occurring! Stand level with the finish line so that you can eliminate players as soon as any part of their body crosses the line (and remember to disqualify any non-movers). Keep going until only one player remains, and declare them the winner! As the winner crosses the line, I like to encourage the group to celebrate the victory – in socially distanced slow motion, of course!

Have a post-race discussion with the 'athletes'... Ask if they had been acutely aware of every part of their body during the exercise? They will invariably answer 'Yes'; by focusing intently on stretching and straining every limb, they will have felt a clear connection to their bodies and to where they were in the space in relation to their rivals. Having this high level of physical connection and spatial awareness is a vital skill for all performers so, out of what is a light-hearted and slightly ridiculous exercise, valuable insight is gained.

# 1-10

**A focus exercise that promotes awareness of the other players.**

Ask all players to find a socially distanced space in the room, and to angle themselves so as to be able to see as many of their fellow players as possible. Now, explain that the aim of the game is to count to ten. 'Easy!' they will cry... well, not quite as easy as they might think!

Players are to call out one number at a time, starting with one and working up to ten (obviously!). Any player can call out a number at any time, *but* – and here comes the tricky bit – if two players say a number at the same time, you must stop the exercise immediately and start over! Keep going until you reach the promised land of the perfect ten... it may take a little while to get there, but it's worth persevering with, as the players will feel a great sense of achievement when they finally reach that uninterrupted landmark.

This exercise encourages players to work as one cohesive unit; a collection of individuals, desperately vying to have their voices heard, will not achieve success here. Players must demonstrate focus, an awareness of the others, and a recognition that everyone has an equal right to contribute. Only by applying these skills will success be achieved.

## Variation: Blind 1-10

Once you have succeeded in counting to an uninterrupted ten, it's time to raise the stakes by asking players to remain in their socially distanced spaces, but this time to lie on their backs, with knees up and eyes closed. It's time to repeat the exercise 'blind'...

Ask that players continue to focus on the others within the group, even with their eyes closed, and to attempt to form a connection with those around them. This added dimension can bring immense focus to the room and with the 'blind', focused silence, you will be amazed at how quickly the challenge can be achieved.

Appetisers

# 1-Minute Focus

> If you have a particularly energetic group, this exercise is a great way of quickly bringing order and calm to proceedings.

Ask the players to find a space which is a safe distance away from their fellow players, and to lie on their backs. When all participants are lying comfortably, ask them to close their eyes and announce that the aim of the game is to count up to one minute (in their heads) and when they think that sixty seconds is up, they are to raise their hand (keeping their eyes closed until you bring the exercise to an end).

So, when everyone is fully focused, give a 'three, two, one' countdown and start the timer!

Keep your eyes on both the stopwatch and the players, and make a note of the time at which the first and last players raise their hands and, of course, which player gets closest to the minute mark. From my experience, there will always be someone who displays fantastic accuracy here. When all hands have been raised, stop the exercise and have all players sit up... announce the player who rose their hand first (along with their time), followed by the one who rose last (along with their time), before revealing the one and only winner!

This is such an effective exercise as it instantly brings a tangible focus to the room and is a great tool for preparing an energetic group for more focused work.

*Note: It is a good idea to remove any ticking clocks from the room before this exercise, as it tends to make counting easier – and promotes foul play!*

Appetisers

# 15

# Pass the Focus

**An exercise requiring players to demonstrate clarity of focus and a strong awareness of the others.**

Ask the players to form a socially distanced audience and ask for five volunteers to take to the playing area. Ask these volunteers to stand in an appropriately spaced line facing the audience, and number them from one to five in sequence from left to right.

This exercise requires a key skill for any performer: knowing where the focus is. For the purpose of this exercise, the focus will initially be on Player 1... You should clarify here exactly what you mean by a player being 'in focus', so explain that, when a player is 'in focus', the gaze, attention and focus of all other players will be firmly fixed in their direction. In this instance, Players 2 to 5 will be focused squarely on Player 1, who should send a neutral gaze out towards the audience. And go...

After Player 1 has been in focus for a little while, change the focus to Player 2... Players 1, 3, 4 and 5 will now turn their focus to Player 2, who will move his/her focus over the audience. Continue this all the way down the line before asking the players to pass the focus back the other way without you calling out their numbers. Encourage the players to remain as still and concentrated as possible and not to 'take focus' when it's not their turn in the spotlight (easier said than done with particularly enthusiastic performers). With such a focused exercise it becomes blindingly obvious if any of the players lose focus at any stage. If, for example, they are all fully focused and extremely still, but one of them scratches their nose, in the absence of any other movement, the focus will immediately be drawn to the nose-scratcher!

When the focus is finally returned to Player 1, bring the exercise to a close and ask the audience who they were looking at during the exercise. The answer will always be: at the player facing the audience. But why is that?... Because, without the audience being aware of it, the performers were purposely framing the player in focus and guiding the audience as to where they should be looking. If the exercise is played effectively, there will be no reason for the audience to look anywhere other than at the player in focus, but if others are fidgeting and gesturing, then they will be confused as to where the focus is. With all this in mind, keep inviting five new players into the playing area until you achieve a perfectly concentrated passing of the focus both down and up the line (it will usually take two or three attempts to perfect this).

This is such a valuable lesson as it shows the importance of players supporting their fellow performers, and demonstrates how the simple act of sending your focus to others can concentrate the attention of the watching audience, and bring a great deal more clarity to dramatic work.

# Ping-Pong Balls

> An enjoyably daft and physical Appetiser devised for younger players to follow instructions, use their imaginations, and expend their energy.

Ask the players to find a socially distanced space in the playing area and to face you. With a straight face ask if they have brought their ping-pong balls with them?! They will probably throw some choice looks your way and say, 'No!' Don't be discouraged by this, just whip out your own (imaginary) ping-pong ball and hold it aloft for all to see! The group will quickly get the idea and 'remember' that they have, in fact, brought their ping-pong balls and will hold them aloft too. If there are still players who continue to insist that they have come empty-handed, proceed to fling ping-pong balls from your (imaginary) collection in their general direction!

Once all players are in possession of their ping-pong balls, ask that they look closely at them. On closer inspection, they will see that there are three tiny zips on each ball. Players should proceed to unzip their ping-pong balls and unfurl them, so that they resemble very small (ping-pong-shaped) peeled bananas. Once unzipped and prised open, instruct the group to place their ping-pong balls on the floor in front of them... Now, here comes the tricky bit: slowly but surely, everyone is going to squeeze their entire body inside their ping-pong ball! You should take the lead with this by initially inserting your big toe into the ping-pong ball and encouraging the group to do the same, next squeeze your whole foot in, then your other big toe and your other foot, then your knees, your shoulders, your head... until you are completely encased within the tiny ball. Once fully curled up inside your ball, it's time to zip yourself up so, taking the lead again, instruct all players to pull the three zips over their bodies until they are fully encased within the ball.

You will now be faced with the not-everyday sight of a group of players crammed into very tiny, very imaginary, fully zipped-up ping-pong balls! Once you have taken in this breathtaking, never-to-be-forgotten sight... it's time to set them free. So, on the count of three, explain that the zips are going to burst open and the group are going to bounce on the spot (or around their room if playing online) as if they have actually become ping-pong balls! And 'Three, two, one – Bounce!'

Once everyone has bounced for a sufficiently long time, bring the exercise to a close and use the energy created to drive the work to come.

# 17 The Puppeteer

An enjoyable physical exercise, which encourages younger players to follow a series of increasingly complex instructions.

Ask the players to sit at a social distance in the playing area facing you. Explain that they are no longer human beings but have become puppets, sitting lifelessly on the toymaker's shelf. Suddenly, the toymaker takes hold of the strings and pulls the puppets to their feet – all players should be encouraged to bring themselves into standing, puppet positions. The toymaker is testing the puppets in order to make sure that they are ready for the toy shop! You will now control the puppets by announcing which strings are being pulled by the toymaker:

★ Left foot up.
★ Left foot down.
★ Right elbow up.
★ Right hand up.
★ Right hand wave.
★ FALL!

Whenever you call 'Fall!', the players must revert to their original collapsed positions before you pick them back up and experiment with other movements.

Once you've pulled ankles, knees, ears, fingers, toes, noses and shoulders... it's time to get the puppets on the move, so have them slowly walk forward:

★ Left foot up, right elbow up.
★ Left foot down, right elbow down.
★ Right foot up, left elbow up.
★ Right foot down, left elbow down.

Players should be encouraged to be acutely aware of every movement in their body and fully connected to each and every gesture as they tentatively walk forward on their string-controlled limbs! Now, try to talk them through hopping or jumping back to their original positions before slumping into their collapsed state.

This is such an effective exercise as you can experiment with and explore a whole range of movements and, by the end of it, limbs will be fully warmed up with players ready to face the next challenge!

# Yes-and-No Game

A classic fun-filled, concentration game for all ages.

Ask the players to form an audience by sitting, socially distanced, around the outer edge of the space. Next, place a chair in the playing area and have one player sit in the chair; it's time for the interrogation to begin!

Explain to the player that they are not, under any circumstances, to use the words 'Yes' or 'No'! Now, start your stopwatch and bombard the 'victim' with a sequence of random questions, such as:

★ Have you ever been to France?

★ Did you like it there?

★ Did you eat a snail?

★ Have you ever ridden a camel?

★ What's your favourite colour?

★ What's the capital of the UK?

★ Are you sure?

★ Can you swim?

★ Are you an alien?

★ Really?

★ Sure about that?!...

The idea is, of course, to try to get the seated player to say 'Yes' or 'No' (or to nod or shake their head). As soon as they do, stop the clock and make a note of the time.

Players facing the interrogation are not permitted to 'plead the fifth' and say nothing... they must answer every question without pausing or hesitating or repeating something over and over! Cool heads and quick thinking are needed here and, as the interrogator, you should do your very best to outwit the seated players by barraging them with as relentless a torrent of questions as possible.

Keep a record of how long each player lasts before cracking under the pressure, so that at the end of the game, when everyone has had a turn, you can announce the champion.

# 19    Blind Obstacle Course

**A focused exercise that requires clarity, teamwork and trust.**

Allocate the players into pairs, whilst keeping a safe distance, and ask them to name one of them 'A' and the other 'B'. Ask all As to sit on one side of the room and all B's to sit on the opposite side (socially distanced, of course). By seating them in this way, you will have created a natural space in which to place your obstacle course. You can use whatever you have at your disposal to create the course, but my obstacle course consists of two chairs, a cone and a beanbag, placed like this:

Call the first pair into the arena and have them decide who is to run the course and who will be the describer. The describer then stands on the finish line, whilst the course runner stands on the start line and places a blindfold over their eyes. The describer's task is to guide the runner through the course; the runner must walk between the chairs, circle the cone, place the beanbag on their head and cross the finish line!

With stopwatch in your hand, ask the runner to spin on the spot twice before announcing that the time starts... NOW! On your 'Go', the describer should shout instructions to the runner! When the runner crosses the finish line after clearing all obstacles correctly, stop the clock and note the time. Call two new volunteers into the arena and, once their blindfold has been donned, rearrange the objects (so that the course is different every time) and restart the challenge. At the end, announce the winners!

The describer must be concise and clear with their instructions, whilst the runner must listen intently, concentrate on the task in hand and put their trust in their fellow player. It's great fun to play, and a great many valuable lessons come from it too.

*Note: If you are going to play this game, then you should ask each member of the group to bring their own blindfold to the session – a scarf or eye mask is fine – so that blindfolds are not shared. You can also bring a supply of your own clean blindfolds, in case anyone forgets, but must wash them following the session.*

# Grandma's Footsteps

A classic game, tweaked for optimal social-distancing.

First of all, choose a player to be Grandma (I usually select the oldest player for this role the first time we play). Once Grandma has been chosen, she should take herself to one end of the room (use the long side of the room to ensure maximum social distancing), whilst the rest of the players line up on the opposite side of the room, like this:

The game is usually played with players closing in on an object that is placed behind Grandma's back, but for the socially distanced version, the object has been replaced with a finish line, as shown above, and the aim of the exercise is to be the first player to cross it. Every time Grandma turns her back on the players, they are permitted to make a dash for the line, but as soon as Grandma turns around, they must immediately *freeze*! If Grandma sees any players moving a muscle, they must be sent back to the start line.

Physical control is all important here; players must balance the desire to get to the finish line with the ability to stop when Grandma turns around – running like a raging bull will rarely get the win in this game. When a player crosses the finish line, declare them the winner – and the prize for winning is to become Grandma! So send the others back to the opposite side of the room and restart the game.

If you're playing online, have players start at the furthest point away from their computer and move towards their screen. The winner is the first player to arrive back at their computer and type 'Winner' in the chat box, without being caught moving.

# Starters

Following an Appetiser or two, the players should be nicely warmed up and ready to move on to the more challenging work ahead: cue the Starters!

These exercises require a little more creative input from the players and are designed to bridge the gap between Appetiser and Main Course. One Starter should suffice, but if you're feeling adventurous (and have time), why not go for two?

# The Mad Hatter's Tea Party

**This high-energy exercise encourages strong character-playing and connection between players.**

**Starters**

First of all, prepare your Tea Party by laying out tables and chairs (or just chairs if you don't have tables) to create the Mad Hatter's banquet, in the following layout:

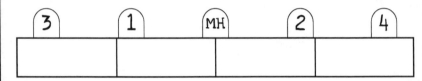

Once set up, choose a player to be the Mad Hatter and invite them to sit on the centre chair before announcing what they are celebrating – remember this is the Mad Hatter's tea party so the reason for the celebration should be suitably zany! Next, ask for four volunteers from the audience and number them from one to four. Explain that, during the exercise, you will make four knocking sounds. On the first knock, Player 1 will enter and sit on chair 1; on the second knock, Player 2 will enter and sit on chair 2; on the third knock... well, I think you get where we're going with this!

As each guest enters, they should possess a larger-than-life personality. This is not a party for the average partygoer, so they should choose and play a distinct characteristic: hugely introverted, massively flamboyant, extremely posh, incredibly anxious... Now – here's the important part – when each guest enters the party, everyone present at the party (including the Hatter) must mimic the characteristics of the arriving guest. If a very angry guest enters the banquet, everyone at the party must become angry too, mimicking the physicality and vocal quality of the new guest as accurately as possible. All guests must stay 'in character' until the Hatter invites a new guest to enter (on hearing your knocking sound); at which point they should switch characters and assume the character traits of the new guest. Whilst playing these larger-than-life characters, players should remember that they are there to celebrate with the Hatter, so they should centre the conversation around the celebration and not just come in wailing, howling, hysterically laughing or whatever. It is quite a challenge to congratulate the Hatter for becoming the world's best time-machine pilot, for instance, whilst hysterically crying or churning with anger – but this juxtaposition of saying one thing and displaying another is what makes this exercise challenging... and often hilarious!

Once all four guests have arrived, you can either bring the exercise to an end or ask Player 4 to leave the party, and have the other players revert back to Player 3's character, before asking Player 3 to exit as the players return to Player 2's character... continuing until all the guests have left and the Hatter is once again alone.

# Sonnet on 1 Breath

A Shakespearean challenge that may take a few weeks, terms or even years to conquer, but it is a very effective tool for improving breath control.

Starters

The challenge is (as you might expect from the title) to recite a sonnet on one breath. I usually use Shakespeare's Sonnet 29 (below), but just can choose your favourite – the Bard did write quite a few!

> When in disgrace with fortune and men's eyes,
> I all alone beweep my outcast state
> And trouble deaf heaven with my bootless cries
> And look upon myself and curse my fate,
> Wishing me like to one more rich in hope,
> Featured like him, like him with friends possess'd,
> Desiring this man's art and that man's scope,
> With what I most enjoy contented least:
> Yet in these thoughts myself almost despising,
> Haply I think on thee, and then my state,
> Like to the lark at break of day arising,
> From sullen earth sings hymns at heaven's gate,
> For thy sweet love remember'd such wealth brings
> That then I scorn to change my state with kings.

Once sonnets have been allocated, it's a good idea to spend a little time discussing the content and getting to know the work in a little more detail – see the modern paraphrasing of this Sonnet in the Resource Pack.

With analysis complete and players familiarised with the work, it's time for the great 'Sonnet on 1 Breath' Challenge! Ask the players to step up, one at a time, take a gargantuan breath and attempt to recite the sonnet without pausing for breath! If a player completes the challenge, they should sit in the playing area; if not, they should return to the audience. When all players have attempted the challenge, make a note of how many players are sat in the playing area and, after weeks of practising breathing exercises, attempt the exercise again. You should find that all players will improve their performance, and a great many more will be sat proudly in the playing area having conquered the challenge!

# Passports

This challenging exercise encourages players to experiment with several continents' worth of accents, often with hilarious results.

Before the session, you should create a number of passports: small, folded documents with a nationality written inside. The nationalities should be as varied as possible, such as Irish, Russian, Spanish, Jamaican, Australian, Swedish... You get the idea. Ensure that you have as many different nationalities as you have players and you are good to go!

Ask the group to form a socially distanced audience and select two volunteers to play out a scene. The scenario for the scene should offer good scope for dramatic exploration whilst keeping the players socially distanced – so someone receiving test results from a doctor; a police officer trying to talk someone down from the ledge; a victim pleading with a kidnapper to set them free, and so on. Before the action unfolds, issue each player with a passport (ensuring that it's folded shut so they can't see their given nationality). Instruct them to keep their passports in hand (or to place them in a pocket), resisting the urge to peek until midway through the scene, when you should clap your hands and call 'Freeze!' On this signal, the players should open their passport to reveal their new nationality. Now, resume the scene, only this time, the players must speak in their new accents! Let the scene play out for a short while (allowing for several moments of unbounded hysteria to ensue!), before bringing the action to a close. It's over to the audience now: can they guess the accents?

Very often, it will be extremely difficult to decipher the origins of each player, but correctly guessing nationalities isn't really the main focus of this exercise. The most important thing is that players show a willingness to throw themselves into the challenge with freedom and joy. When faced with accent work, players often feel self-conscious and worry about sounding silly. By presenting it in this relaxed and fun way, they will feel much more open to try and will frequently be surprised by just how adept at accent work they are.

Ask for two more volunteers – there will invariably be a sea of eager hands at this point – choose a new scenario, allocate new passports... and go again!

The more you play, the more players will leave ego aside and be able to throw themselves with gusto into acting with their new accents. Suddenly, accent work will become a lot less daunting, and the fun to be had in learning will make it a highly addictive (and much requested) exercise!

*Note: If playing online, when you freeze the scene, ask everyone to close their eyes and show the performers (in turn) their passports. When accents have been received, everyone should reopen their eyes and resume the playing! At the end of the exercise, ask all of the group to type in the chat box what they thought the two accents were.*

# Challenge Chair

**Remaining calm, focused and composed under pressure is on the menu with this quick-fire Starter.**

Ask the players to form a socially distanced audience (in the round works well) and place a single chair in the centre of the playing area. Next, invite all players, in turn, to enter the playing area and to sit on the 'Challenge Chair'. Once seated, they are to be given ten seconds to name as many items as they can from a given subject. These subjects can be as varied as you can conjure: farmyard animals, football teams, shops, things you find in a fridge, school subjects, modes of transport, artists, chocolate bars, ways to become a millionaire... Let your imagination go wild! Keep a tally of the scores as you go along, and after all players have been challenged... announce the overall Challenge Chair Champion! In the event of a tie, hold a Challenge Chair play-off between the tied competitors.

Once you've played the individual version, it's time to introduce a team-playing element to the challenge by asking players to compete in small groups. Place three challenge chairs in a socially distanced line in the playing area (or more if you want to play with bigger teams).

Now, invite a team of three to sit and, this time, the contestants must take it in turns to give one answer each – but if a contestant repeats a given answer, all points for that round will be lost. This is a very effective variation as it encourages teamwork and listening. Once again, keep a tally of the points scored, so that you can announce the winning team at the end.

*Note: When working with teams and increasing the number of challenge chairs, it is a good idea to increase the time limit too – so for three players, set a time limit of thirty seconds, and so on.*

# Confession Time

**Truth, focus, staying in the moment and building a narrative are required in this often-impactful Starter.**

First of all, you should create your confessional booth. There are two options available here: either two chairs side by side with a central partition, so that the players can't see each other, or two chairs back to back, which works best with the audience in the round.

Now, invite one player to sit on a chair – they will be the listener to the confession – and another player to be the confessor. Before entering the confessional chair, players should think of a suitably regrettable act that they have committed. Better to keep it light-hearted and fictional! The offence can be anything at all, as long as they feel deep shame for their actions and are prepared to fully repent in the booth! On entering the booth, the confessor must state: 'Forgive me, for I have sinned.'

What will follow is a thirty-second conversation between the listener and the confessor as the true magnitude of what they have done is laid out. The confession shouldn't be immediately blurted out, but gradually revealed as the player shows ever-increasing remorse for their actions. Truth is important here; the confessor must place themselves firmly in the shoes of the offender and show true regret for their actions.

The role of the listener is key here. Although, at first sight, it may seem like a passive role, the listener is responsible for driving the narrative forwards and bringing maximum impact to the work. Listeners should take on board the initial confession, consider what additional information is required (to add additional interest to the confession) and use questioning to steer the journey of the confession. By asking probing questions, listeners will get to the very heart of the story and prevent confessors from bringing half-hearted or unconsidered confessions to the booth!

This is difficult to achieve in such a short time-scale with such little preparation, so focus, commitment and a willingness to immerse themselves in the created world are vital. Once the full confession has been made, the listener should offer their advice and/or punishment for the crime! After this, the confessor will become the listener; a new confessor will enter the booth and a brand-new confession is made. Continue this until all players have had a turn at both confessing and listening.

This exercise can very often enter into the realms of the absurd, and some players will find it hard to keep a straight face as they confess, but there will always be two or three extremely powerful and impactful moments produced from this premise.

# Do Quote Me

Many performers fall into the trap of learning lines by desperately cramming words into their short-term memory. This exercise sets out to prove that such a practice is flawed and that, when placed under pressure (as performers often are), those hastily learnt lines will often vanish into the ether!

Before the session, you should prepare a number of dramatic quote-cards (pieces of card with famous quotes from plays or films written upon them); you will need as many quote-cards as you have performers and each quote must be individually numbered. Here are some examples:

1.  'When you realise you want to spend the rest of your life with somebody, you want the rest of your life to start as soon as possible.'

2.  'If you let my daughter go now, that'll be the end of it. But if you don't, I will look for you, I will find you, and I will kill you.'

Ask the group to form an audience in the round and distribute one quote-card to each player, ensuring that you have the master document (with all the numbered quotes) to hand. Players have just one minute to learn their lines so, eyes down and... let the line-learning commence!

Following an intense minute of desperate quote-cramming, call a halt to proceedings and collect in the quote-cards. Now, it's time to see how well they got on – but before you do, it's always a good idea to throw in a curveball exercise – something like *1-Minute Focus* ought to do it. This will add to the challenge and really test how deeply they have learnt their lines by putting time between the line-learning and the reciting. So – curveball exercise played – it's time to recite some quotes!

Checking against your master document, invite the person who had quote-card 1 to enter the playing area and recite their given quote. Keep a close eye on the master document: if they make a single mistake (no matter how small), stop the recital immediately and ask the player to return to the audience. If a player manages to recite their quote correctly, they should remain in the playing area and sit. Continue this process until everyone has attempted the challenge and count up how many players are sitting in the playing area – maybe just over half (if you're lucky). So, how are you going to improve on this?

Ask all players to return to the audience and redistribute the quotes, ensuring that players are given a different one this time, along with a pen or a pencil... it's time for a new approach! First of all, have everyone read their quotes out loud several times, before asking them to underline three words that they feel need emphasising. Next, they should draw three symbols next to three words: smiley faces, balloons, a ball of flames... anything at all, as long as it relates to the word and is memorable to them. Finally, ask that they continually speak their lines whilst bringing different qualities to the recital; first whispered, then excitedly, then terrified, then angrily... as many variations as possible, so that several possibilities within the text are realised.

Finally, collect up the quotes and restart the recital. You will find that many more players are sat in the playing area by the end of this second round, proving that the way players learn their lines directly affects their ability not only to retain them but also to deliver them with truth, colour, interest and dynamism.

# 30-Second Story

The ability to remain immersed in the created world when faced with an expectant audience is a key skill for any performer and this exercise puts that skill firmly to the test.

For this storytelling challenge, you will need a number of storybooks with as many titles as you have players so, before the session begins, you should get creative and produce several never-before-read blockbuster-story titles by folding sheets of A5 card and writing a different title on each cover (leaving the centre pages blank). These titles should be catchy, dramatic and evocative, like the following:

★ *The Ghost Ship*
★ *Escape from Dinosaur Island*
★ *The Cave of DOOM*

Armed with your blockbuster books, ask the players to form an audience in the round and place a single chair in the playing area. This is the storytelling chair so make sure it's as comfy as possible! Ask a player to sit in the chair, before presenting them with a 'book' and asking them to read the title out loud… Once they've announced the title, explain that they have thirty seconds to read an engaging passage from the book. The operative word here is 'engaging' – with such limited time to tell the tale, they should cut out any preamble and head directly to the meat of the story, throwing the audience into the very heart of the action from the get-go. Of course, upon closer inspection, players will find that the centre pages are, in fact, blank; that is because the story must be produced entirely from their imaginations… so, grab your stopwatch and announce that 'Thirty seconds start… NOW!'

Thirty seconds doesn't seem such a long time until you are sat, blank book in hand, with an expectant audience waiting to be entertained… and in these circumstances, thirty seconds will feel a whole lot longer! The trick is to shut out the gaze of the audience and to become fully submerged in the created world. Readers should be encouraged to stay as relaxed as possible, to open up their imaginations, and to relay the tale with as much truth and colour as they can. This exercise is not about dazzling the audience with dynamic wordplay, but about becoming immersed in another world and painting a truthful picture of it. The more immersed they become, the more they will forget about the watching audience, and the more vivid and dynamic the dramatic tale will be. The audience will instinctively know the difference between a player who is seeing and conveying a world from their mind's eye and one who is trying desperately to fill the time, so every effort should be made by the storyteller to be in the moment and connected to the story.

This exercise always throws up a wide array of outcomes, from grippingly intense to totally lost for words! With continued play, players will become increasingly comfortable and adept at allowing the contents of their creative minds to flow with confidence, creativity and conviction.

# The Translator

An interactive and focused exercise that encourages players to listen and connect with their fellow performers.

Ask the players to form an audience and place three chairs in the playing area like below:

A

B ←→ 2m ←→ (chair) ←→ 2m ←→ C

Next, ask for three volunteers to sit in the three chairs. Once they are sitting comfortably, inform the player in chair C that they are here for a job interview and that the player in chair B is the company boss who will be conducting today's interview. But this will not be a straightforward job interview, since the boss is from a faraway place with a language all of its own. They will be firmly reliant on the translator (the player in chair A) to ensure that the interview goes smoothly.

In order to decide upon the nature of the job, it's a good idea to take suggestions from the audience; this way you'll get a broad (and often wacky) range of job titles to choose from: America's next top model... lion tamer... cat-food taster... Let's go with lion tamer! With the occupation established, reiterate that the boss must speak in gibberish for the entire interview with strictly no use of their native tongue at all. Instruct the boss to ask the first question and, once they've muttered some indecipherable gibberish, ask the translator to translate the gibberish into English for the candidate. When the candidate replies, the translator should then translate the reply back into gibberish for the boss, trying their best to use the same 'language'. The translator should watch the boss carefully and do their best to get the general gist of the question before relaying it to the interviewer. Encourage the boss to be both physically and vocally engaging so that the translator has plenty to work with; if they monotonously drone out their questioning with no gesture or vocal colour, it will be extremely difficult for the translator to get a flavour of what it is they wish to ask the candidate.

Allow the interview to play out for a while before bringing it to a close, and have a post-interview discussion about how well the players worked together to complete the task. Did they listen carefully? Did they use the same 'language'? Did the boss help the translator by providing colour and physical gesture to the questioning? Does the candidate get the job?! When the debrief is over, choose three new players, a brand-new job title, an all-new language, and start over!

This exercise is all about awareness of the others. Success can only be achieved by working closely with your fellow performers so, even though this exercise is fun (and often ridiculous), there is a valuable lesson underpinning its playing.

## 29

# Call Connection

This exercise encourages players to immerse themselves physically in the narrative and to bring purpose and drive to their movement.

Ask the players to form a socially distanced audience – a thrust audience (on three sides) works well. Place a table in the playing area and ask for a volunteer to place their phone (turned off!) on the table and to step outside the playing area (as far away from the table as possible). Explain that the phone is going to ring, and when it does, they should re-enter the playing area and answer it. Play a sound effect of a ringing phone, and when the player arrives at the phone and picks it up... freeze the action immediately! Ask the audience what they have learned about this character. Well, nothing much, apart from the fact that they can answer a phone!

They have, in truth, done exactly as they were asked: crossed to the phone and answered it... but is it enough for a performer merely to enter a space and perform a directed task? The answer is, of course, no! Players must bring *something* into the playing area (and by 'something' I mean purpose, drive, motivation, emotion, focus). To emphasise this point, ask another player to enter the playing area and place their phone on the table but this time, before the phone rings, they should pick a focus card from the envelope which you will have prepared before the session began... These focus cards provide a variety of motivations designed to drive the players as they enter and answer the phone. Here are some examples:

★ Expecting *sad* news.
★ *Nervous* about the call.
★ Expecting *happy* news.
★ *Worried* about what is going to be said.
★ *Furious* with the caller.
★ *Terrified* about answering.

Let's say that a player chooses the card instructing them to be 'Nervous about the call'. Firstly, ask that they keep the information on the card to themselves, so that the audience don't know their motivation. Secondly, allow them a moment to consider *why* they are so nervous about taking this particular phone call. Once their motivation is clear, stand by and activate the phone ringing...

**CONTINUED...**

The player will approach the phone as before, only this time there should be a stark contrast in the quality of movement – where once there was a lack of focus, there will now be a clear purpose and drive underpinning the movement. When the player arrives at the phone and accepts the call... freeze the action. Now it's over to the audience: can they guess the focus? In many cases, the answer will be 'Yes', because even without saying a word, a clear sense of nervousness and tension will have been conveyed as the player tentatively approached the phone. Once you've received the verdict from the audience, it's time to restart the action to see if they were right, so the player in focus must now take the call to confirm (or otherwise) the audience's suspicions. After thirty seconds or so (depending on how engaging it is), bring the conversation to a close, confirm the focus and ask for another player to take to the stage with a new focus.

This is such a valuable lesson as it shows just how much an audience can glean from a performance, long before any words have been uttered. Performers should always strive to allow their focus and motivation to drive their movements and actions; this way, they will bring something dynamic into the space and their work will be filled with clarity, purpose and interest.

*Note: If playing online, ask all other players to close their eyes as you display the motivation to the player. The phone should be placed (or imagined) by their screen, and the player should move as far away as possible from the screen before moving towards it to answer the phone.*

★

# 30

# Picture Perfect

This focused Starter is an effective tool for improving descriptive and communication skills.

Before the session, prepare a pack of Picture-Perfect Printouts (that's a keeper for a future tongue-twister exercise)! A Picture-Perfect Printout is a sheet of A4 paper with twelve recognisable objects (cut out of magazines or downloaded from the internet); see examples in the Resource Pack.

Armed with your Picture-Perfect Printouts, instruct the group to pair up and to find a suitably distanced space and sit back to back. Next, circulate the room and place one Picture-Perfect Printout, face down, in front of one member of each pair – that person is the describer for round one. On your command, the describer should turn the paper over and they have one minute to describe each object to their partner, e.g. 'It's yellow with four wheels and transports children to school'... No, not a Lamborghini; a school bus! The guessers must, at all costs, resist the urge to take a sneaky peek over their shoulder and should attempt to name as many of the described objects as possible within an allocated time. So, with rules clear, it's time to start the describing – and... GO!

On your signal, the room will burst into life as players desperately try to describe the twelve objects in the allocated time. After giving a ten-second countdown (to add to the tension!), bring the exercise to a close and find out how many pairs managed to guess all twelve – probably not many, in fact; most will have come some way short. So, how do we improve on this for round two?

★ Use more accurate and descriptive adjectives.

★ Speak more clearly.

★ Project your voice when describing.

★ Listen more intently.

★ Focus fully on your partner.

★ Don't allow yourself to be distracted by others.

It's amazing how many valuable lessons can emerge from this one, simple exercise. Give a new Picture-Perfect Printout to each pair, and the describers from the first round now become the listeners/guessers – and GO! After the discussion, you will find that mostly all participants will have improved on their first-round score and many will have reached the promised land of the perfect twelve!

# Imaginary Journey

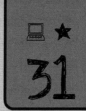

An inclusive group exercise that encourages performers to release their imaginations and explore (and believe in) a created world.

Ask the players to find a space in the room, suitably distanced from their fellow players, and to lie on their backs, close their eyes and relax. They are about to be taken on an imaginary journey with you as their guide. There are no boundaries to where you can go or what can happen on this journey; the players must simply relax, listen to your instructions, and immerse themselves as deeply as possible in the created world.

You might start the journey on a beach, instructing all players to feel the sweltering sun beating down on their faces before taking a walk over the hot sand and dipping their toes in the ice-cold water... Behind them, they see a sheer cliff face – they decide to climb it and, as they reach the top, before them is lush greenery for as far as the eye can see... They walk through the long grass and in the distance they see a strange-looking house... They walk towards the house and find a secret way in... Once inside, they climb the stairs, and find an unusual wardrobe... They open it and find a mysterious box... They discover an unusual object inside the box... Suddenly, they hear a scary noise! They run out of the house, and hide in the long grass... The noise slowly subsides as they fall fast asleep, listening to the sound of the grass blowing in the breeze... When they wake up, they are back in their drama session, and should sit up carefully!

At the end of the exercise, ask some questions to explore what the group were imagining. For instance, with the story above: What was strange about the house? What was unusual about the wardrobe? What was inside the box? What was scary about the noise?... You will find that you are greeted with a myriad of weird and wonderful answers – and you can congratulate the group for using their actors' imaginations: that unique ability to picture and believe in an imagined world. Many players will speak with such certainty and clarity as if they have actually been to the beach, climbed the cliff, visited the house, opened the box... This ability to place themselves within a fantasy must be hugely applauded.

This is an excellent Starter to fire the originality and invention of the players, and it is a joy to watch them submerge themselves deeply within their imaginations. It is also a useful tool for bringing focus to a particularly exuberant group. Enjoy the journey!

# 32

# Speed Hate

Love is most definitely not on the menu in this fun-filled play on a speed-date scenario.

Ask the players to form an audience in the round, and place two chairs at a distance apart in the playing area. Now, encourage one eager participant to sit on a chair and then explain that they are about to go on a date... in fact, everyone's going dating! As a look of horror starts on several faces, quickly explain that these will be no ordinary dates – they will be 'speed dates', and, as you may have surmised from the title of the exercise, love is certainly not on the menu. These will be some of the worst speed-dating experiences... ever!

Each player is to be given a twenty-second opportunity to woo their speed-date partner. However, they must create a character so vile, so repugnant, so dull, so weird, so nauseating, that no sane human being would ever fall for them. Ask a player to go first as the awful character, and invite them to the playing space, insisting that they remain seated on the second chair for the full twenty seconds. It could be tempting to get up close and personal with their date, but they must resist that temptation and try to impress from afar! Once the speed date has timed out, ask the initial seated player to rejoin the audience and for the character creator to assume a more normal guise, as they prepare to receive the advances of a brand-new, larger-than-life and equally repulsive character. This will now play like a chain exercise, with each player having the opportunity to create a character, as well as to be on the receiving end of a disastrous date.

Once all dates have played out, discuss which characters were particularly memorable and why. You will usually find that many participants played a little too safe with their character choices and, as a result, you will have witnessed several shy, awkward dates but not quite the 'worst date ever'. So, it's time to go again, only this time, players should attempt to push the limits of their creativity and go the extra mile with their creation: the louder, stranger, angrier, bigger, bolder the characters, the better! In order to help achieve this goal, reduce the time to just five seconds – you will often find that this releases the players' creativity as they will feel free to let go fully, safe in the knowledge that the experience will be very short-lived. The five-second speed round will often produce some fantastically creative and energised work that will leave the players uplifted and enthused.

End the exercise with a discussion about the importance of pushing boundaries during improvisation. It is only by exploring and experimenting with the extremes of characterisation that actors can discover the full range of their performing potential.

# Photographic Memory

**This exercise encourages players to make interesting dramatic choices and to believe in a created reality.**

Before the session, prepare a set of photographs, enough for each member of the group to have one each. Photos from the internet or magazines are fine, and can be of anything: family portraits, boats, cars, landscapes, wildlife... Keep sourcing and printing until you have enough images to go around and no one has to share.

Ask the players to sit in a distanced circle (using chairs if you have them) and allocate one photograph to each player. Explain that the photo in their hand is of great sentimental value to them; in fact, it is the most precious image that they possess and they have brought it along today to share its story with the group. (Of course, this isn't true – you cut them out from a magazine about an hour ago – but for the purposes of this exercise, this is their truth.) Give a few moments for the players to digest their images, asking them to consider what/who is in the image and why it is so important to them. They must try to give as much history to the photo as possible. Information is key here; the more information they have, the more they will have to focus on when telling their story to the group.

Now, it's time to navigate the circle and ask all players, in turn, to reveal their photograph and explain why it is so special to them. There are no time constraints here, players should talk for as long as they wish in order to give the group a good understanding of why it is such an important image to them.

You will often find that the first to show and tell will be a little non-committal and rushed in their delivery, which leads to a lack of truth in the tale. Explain that, for success, players must focus on the history of the image, believe in that history, and immerse themselves as deeply as possible in the created truth. It can take a leap of faith for a performer to engage themselves in this way, but the rewards are huge. If a player believes in the truth of the photograph, the audience will be drawn in too. The deeper into the world they fall, the more immersive and impactful an experience it will be for both performer and audience alike.

As you go around the circle, you will find that players become increasingly prepared to delve deeper into the created world, and you should find that some incredibly powerful, focused and truthful work emerges from this very simple premise.

*Note: If playing online, give players a couple of minutes to find an image themselves that they wish to share with the group – but insist that is from a book or magazine. It cannot be from a family album, since that genuinely will mean something to them and therefore defeat the object of the exercise!*

# 34

# Outside In

**A focused Starter that encourages truth and focus in performance.**

Ask the players to form a semicircular (and adequately distanced) audience facing a door. Next, request a volunteer and explain that they are going to exit through the door and re-enter in response to something dramatic that has just happened outside. Give a few examples of what could have conceivably happened out there to get the creative juices flowing, such as:

★ You were chased by the police.

★ You have just returned from a perfect first date.

★ You have just been dumped.

★ You are returning from a drunken night out.

★ You just witnessed an alien spaceship land.

Ask the chosen player to step outside, close the door and then re-enter when ready, and for the audience to remain silent, focused and respectful during the performance.

What you will probably find is that, for the first few attempts, entering players will lack conviction, will be a little too aware of the watching audience and will resort to 'acting' as opposed to believing in a created reality. Discourage this approach by asking that players trust their instincts and explaining that the audience will be with them even if they are not being 'performed' to... Explain that it is much more engaging for an audience to feel that they are a fly on the wall watching something unfold, rather than being explicitly told or shown what to feel or think.

Encourage them to begin the work outside the door, rather than when players enter the space. Whilst outside, players should give themselves information, focus on that information and be 'in the moment' *before* they reach for the door handle. This approach will reap untold benefits and will see each player bring something different and dynamic into the playing area, sustaining their focus throughout the exercise.

The more you play, the more the players will take the pressure to 'perform' off their shoulders until they simply allow themselves to believe in and inhabit their new reality. It is a leap of faith to take, but an extremely important one; the audience will attest to the fact that such an approach brings about much more engaging, effective and dramatic work. From the simple act of entering a room, a great many lessons can be learnt.

# Listening Pictures

**A unique exercise that highlights the importance of listening.**

Starters

Before the session, you should draw a series of geometric shapes onto pieces of paper, like this:

With your random shapes in hand, ask the players to pair up, find a (socially distanced) space and sit back to back whilst you circulate the room and place a sheet face down in front of one member of each pair. Next, recirculate the room and distribute blank pieces of paper (the same size as the shape sheets) and pens to their partners. The aim of the exercise is for the player with the sheet to describe the shape, whilst their partners draw it on their blank pieces of paper. Set a time limit of ninety seconds and insist that all players resist the temptation to turn around and have a sneak peek! So, lift up the papers and... Go!

When the time is up, stop the exercise and let the players inspect their work. Often, the resemblance between the two papers will be fleeting at best! Have a discussion about how things could be improved, such as:

★ Listen more closely.

★ Speak more clearly.

★ Give more precise information about the size/position of the objects (and orientation of the paper).

★ Block out the sound of the other members of the group and focus exclusively on your partner.

After the discussion, switch the partners around, and give each pair a new sheet – and then run the exercise again. You should find a real improvement the second time around as they apply the skills highlighted in the discussion.

# The Memory Test

**A very effective concentration game that will focus minds towards the beginning of a session.**

Before the session, prepare a series of Memory Test sheets, with sixteen recognisable and random objects (cut out of magazines or downloaded from the internet). Each sheet should be numbered and have its own unique combination of objects; see examples in the Resource Pack.

Ask the players to pair up, find a (socially distanced) space, and sit down. Once seated, hand out one Memory Test, face down, to each pair. The aim of the exercise is for players to memorise as many objects as possible (in order, from left to right) in ninety seconds. Players should take it in turns to name and memorise the object so, in the example of Memory Test 1, players would memorise the objects as follows: Player 1 – tin can; Player 2 – paper clip; Player 1 – CD; Player 2 – dog... and so on.

With your stopwatch at the ready, it's time to start the exercise... As players cram the images into their minds, it's a good idea to ramp up the pressure by calling out 'Thirty seconds to go', 'Ten seconds to go', until you give a five-second countdown – and ask all groups to turn their papers face down again. Next, place two distanced chairs in the playing area and ask the players to form an audience (in the round). Now, take a Memory Test at random, call out the number and ask the corresponding pair to take to the stage and to sit on the chairs. They must now recall and recite as many objects as they can from their sheet. Follow your own copy of the sheet carefully and if they make a mistake, stop the exercise, count up the number of objects named and invite the next pair onto the stage. Continue this until all pairs have played and the winning team is declared!

You will often find that later groups are much less likely to remember all the objects; this is because they have crammed an unconnected collection of images into their minds and when put under pressure to recall and recite, the images have been lost in the fog of short-term memory! This is a valuable lesson when it comes to learning lines, demonstrating that cramming words, without thought, context or feeling is ineffective. If players learn dramatic dialogue in this way, their acting will more than likely be wooden and untruthful – and once the pressure of performance falls upon them, they are very likely to forget their lines!

Replay the exercise, only this time, ask the players to create a narrative to help them remember the objects – for example: 'I saw a SHELL on a beach whilst listening to a CD, when a CHICK ran by with a CRAB in its beak!' By connecting images in this way (as opposed to learning a series of unconnected words) the players will learn that context makes a big difference to remembering lines.

# What Happens Next?

A team-playing exercise to encourage creative thinking and explore dramatic structure.

Ask the players to form an audience (in the round), and ask for one volunteer to enter the playing area. What happens to this volunteer over the next couple of minutes will be entirely dependent on the creativity of the gathered audience so, first up, ask for an opening scenario... Who is this person?... Where are they?... What are they doing? This needn't be highly dramatic; it can be as simple as 'It's a young girl walking on a beach.'

With the opening gambit chosen, have the player move around the space, feeling the sea air rushing through her hair. After this has played out for a few moments, freeze the action and ask the audience: What happens next? You should be greeted by a number of suggestions... she gets nipped by a crab... she falls into the sea... she finds a map... Choose the suggestion that you feel will progress the narrative the most and have the player act out the chosen scenario. So, she's found a map... What next?... She follows it to where X marks the spot!... What next?... She digs for treasure... What next?... She finds a buried mobile phone... What next?... The phone rings... You get the idea! Continue taking suggestions until the narrative comes to a dramatic conclusion or the story has run its course.

Encourage the audience to be as creative as possible with their suggestions and to think of ideas that drive the narrative forward. When ideas are fired your way, it's important to explain why it is that you have chosen one idea over another, so that players gain an understanding of what is required to structure a progressive, dynamic and engaging narrative. Outside-the-box thinking is to be celebrated, so urge the players to push the boundaries of what is possible when they consider what happens next, and ask the player in focus to accept every offer and to throw themselves wholeheartedly into the truth of the narrative.

This is such an effective exercise, with players quickly tuning in to what constitutes a scenario ripe for dramatic encounter and what suggestions are just plain dull. Within two or three rounds, the suggestions will be increasingly progressive and the action increasingly dramatic. This clearly demonstrates that players are only limited by their imaginations as to what can be created in the playing area. If they can imagine it and have the courage to believe in it, anything can be created.

# Create a Space

A mime exercise that encourages players to use their imaginations to visualise a created world.

Ask the players to form an audience (in the round), and explain that you're all going to work together to create an imaginary room in the playing area. You should go first in order to get the ball rolling and, as you demonstrate the concept, you should encourage the players to watch carefully. The first thing to create is the door to the room, so decide where (in the playing area) the door is situated, approach it, turn the handle and... enter the 'room'. Once in the room, it's time to create something; this could be a coat stand that you hang your coat on or a sink that you wash your hands in... let's go with the sink idea! Decide where the sink is situated, approach it, turn on the tap and wash away. Once suitably clean, it's time to exit the room through the created door, which should be shut behind you. The door and sink have now been created, and they cannot be uncreated.

Next, ask for a volunteer to enter the space and explain that they must enter through the created door, use one object that already exists, before creating another and exiting. So far, all that has been created in the room is a sink, so the first player to enter after you must use the created sink as well as 'installing' their own object... let's say they watch some television for a while before washing their hands and exiting. The door, sink and now television have been created and cannot be uncreated... The next player to enter through the door will have the option to use the sink *or* the television, as well as creating their own object... and this continues until all players have entered the room, used an object, and created a new one.

Police the miming very carefully so that the door and created objects don't move or change size – and ensure that players don't walk through any of them! After a couple of attempts, the focus in the room will be palpable and the players will be able to visualise the space clearly, although they are actually watching and walking into an empty playing area. Believing in a created reality is a key skill for performers, and this exercise demonstrates that if performers believe in and visualise a created space, the audience will see it too.

# Call It an End

This exercise encourages players to work together, to listen and to connect emotionally in performance.

First of all, place two chairs, some distance apart, in the playing area and ask the players to form a socially distanced audience around the chairs.

Next, ask for two volunteers to sit on the chairs and ask that they bring their (turned-off) mobile phones with them. Once seated, explain that one of the players is going to end something with the other over the phone: this could be a friendship, a relationship, a working partnership... Select one of the players to be the bringer of the news, and explain that the receiver has no idea what's coming and they don't want (whatever it is) to end. Ask that the players gradually build the conversation and work up to the dramatic 'ending'; blurting out 'It's over' as soon as the receiver answers the call will not provide the required drama! Stand by with a sound effect of a ringing phone – and let the dramatic ending begin.

Players will quickly discover that choices are all important here... 'I want to end my phone contract' will have much less impact than 'I want to end our marriage'! With this in mind, players should be urged to choose a dramatic scenario and dare to place themselves firmly in the narrative. If players are prepared to bring truth, passion and emotion to the playing, some extremely intense and engaging theatre can be created from this premise.

Once you've experimented with a few improvised endings, it's time to bring a little more structure to the play by allocating players into pairs based on who they're sitting next to in the audience. Ask each pair to discuss who they are, what is ending and why, before taking to the playing area. Players should heed the lessons of the first round and ensure that their choices offer plenty of scope for emotional connection and dramatic escalation before taking to the stage. This second round is well worth attempting as it will always produce powerful, connected and dynamic work.

# To Bean or Not to Bean

**Starters**

Allowing emotion to colour dialogue is on the menu in this 'pulsating' exercise!

For this exercise, you will need the instructions for cooking baked beans. In case you're wondering how to cook the perfect batch of beans, here are some instructions that I prepared earlier:

'Empty the beans into a saucepan and stir gently whilst heating. Do not boil or overcook as this will impair the flavour.'

These instructions should be placed on a lectern in the centre of the playing area, and ask the players to form a suitably distanced audience around the lectern. You should now take to the stage and announce that you have sourced a magnificent script for today's drama session and, as they wait with bated breath for a performance of Shakespearean proportions, read aloud the bean-cooking instructions! You will be faced by looks of pure bewilderment, but ignore these. Explain that each player is to approach the lectern in turn and, when in place, you will show them an emotion card (being sure not to let anyone else see). Once they have received their given emotion, they should read the cooking instructions using that single, strong emotion to drive their delivery. Some examples of suitable emotions are:

| | | |
|---|---|---|
| EXCITED | SCARED | NERVOUS |
| ANGRY | AMAZED | DELIGHTED |
| CONFUSED | DISAPPOINTED | IN LOVE |
| DISGUSTED | PANIC-STRICKEN | HEARTBROKEN |
| DEPRESSED | BITTER | TERRIFIED |
| AMUSED | PETRIFIED | CONFIDENT |

Players should be encouraged to bring as much vocal and physical attack to the delivery as possible and to fully commit to their emotion.

Now, sit back and watch as the players cry, wail, scream and shout their way through the bean instructions! Keep encouraging them to feel the emotion, allowing it to flow through the words. After all players has delivered their short speech, it will be abundantly clear that any simple 'script' can be delivered in infinitely different ways. Ask if the rest of the group can guess the emotion from those few simple instructions.

This is such an effective exercise as, although slightly ridiculous, it clearly demonstrates that it is the choices we make that colour the spoken word. If players make no choices and just read dialogue aloud, then their vocal delivery will be one-dimensional and dull. But if they dare to feel and inject emotion into their work, they will discover that the possibilities locked within text are limitless – it is just up to the performer to draw them out.

*Note: If playing online, the script can remain in the main chat window for players to read. You can also send them their emotion as a private chat message.*

# Main Courses

With the session in full flow, it's time to move on to the most challenging and creative course of them all – bring on the Mains! These highly creative exercises and games demand maximum input from players and minimal coaching from leaders, so it's time to take a step back and allow the players free rein to create, devise and do what they do best: perform!

The majority of the Main Courses have been devised with the challenge of the physical classroom in mind, but there are still a number of exercises that can be employed effectively in an online setting. With suitably mature players, it's a good idea to use 'breakout rooms' for more structured work, and I would recommend that you continually monitor the activity within these rooms to ensure that they are being used for creative exploration (and not as an excuse for a gossip)!

# 41 Staging by Numbers

This exercise encourages players to bring precision, clarity and purpose to their stage movements.

Before the session, prepare several Staging by Numbers sheets. These are printouts with a number of simple stage directions listed upon them; it's a good idea to prepare two versions, one for groups of two and one for groups of three (as you will rarely have an even number of players in every class). Here's an example for three players:

1.  A enters upstage-right and sits on a chair downstage-left with head in hands.

2.  B enters upstage-left and sits on a chair downstage-right with arms folded.

3.  C enters upstage-right and stands (in second position) upstage-centre.

4.  A stands on their chair.

5.  B stands on their chair.

6.  C walks downstage-centre.

7.  A exits hurriedly upstage-left.

8.  C sits downstage-left.

9.  B climbs down from their chair and moves slowly downstage-centre.

10. C takes something from their pocket.

11. B collapses to the floor.

12. C exits upstage-right.

Every single stage movement is mapped out, making this an extremely useful tool for keeping players suitably distanced in performance.

Before you start the exercise, have a quick recap of stage terminology (if required) by having the group form a socially distanced audience and asking a volunteer to stand upstage-centre, then another to stand downstage-left, then another centre-left and so on, until you have explored every area of the stage... Remember that stage left and right refer to left and rights from the perspective of the actors on stage, *not* the audience. Inexperienced players may need some

CONTINUED...

assistance along the way, so ensure that you assist with this orientation and when you are fully satisfied that all players are up to speed, it's time to begin!

Divide the players into groups of two or three, allocate a Staging by Numbers sheet to each group, and ask them to prepare a scene that precisely follows the given stage directions. They should endeavour to create a storyline that fits the blocking as neatly as possible, and make sure that there is a very definite reason for each movement. Moving for the sake of moving will not do here; there must be a clear, considered driving force behind each and every gesture and move.

Players very often gain confidence from working within such the tight parameters and, although at a distance, this premise can produce dynamic, connected and engaging work.

| RIGHT | | | LEFT |
|---|---|---|---|
| | USR | UPSTAGE<br>USC | USL |
| | CSR | CENTRE STAGE | CSL |
| | DSR | DSC<br>DOWNSTAGE | DSL |

AUDIENCE

# The Power

Creative thinking and commitment in performance are on the menu here. To succeed, players must work closely together and bring strong focus to the playing area.

In theatre, so much of the drama and tension comes from power-play, so this exercise asks that players consider the impact of power in performance. Players are challenged to show greater awareness of the power struggle between characters and to think about how to assert power without physically manhandling their fellow performers to the ground! By asserting power in more nuanced ways, a more complex and convincing performance is achieved.

Divide the players into pairs and ask them to sit in a socially distanced space. Once seated, ask that they decide who will possess 'The Power' and who will be subjected to it. They must devise a short piece that starts with the powerless player waking up in a room – they don't know where they are or why they are there, and there does not seem to be a way out. As they reach the edge of despair, the powerful character enters and the reason for the powerless character's predicament is gradually revealed.

Having such an open premise is a catalyst for creativity; the room can be anywhere and the powerful performer anyone, which opens up massive scope for drama. It could be a concentration camp and the powerful character is the officer in charge, a dental practice with a particularly sadistic dentist, or the waiting room for Hell presided over by the Devil himself! Creative thinking is to be encouraged in order to make the piece as engaging and tense as possible.

Ask that the powerful player fully embodies the role and commits to their power. There should be a feeling that they are toying with the weaker player and very much enjoying the feeling that having a psychological advantage over the other brings. Players should also consider carefully the staging of the piece. Positioning players upstage can give them presence and power, and using different physical levels can be an effective tool in displaying who has control over the situation. Insist that at no stage can a performer be within two metres of the other – power must always be asserted from a distance.

This premise never fails to produce impactful, engaging and at times utterly creepy performance pieces. Thinking outside the box – and finding alternative ways to display dominance, authority and power – will create considered, connected work.

# Two Sides to Every Story

Creative thinking and commitment in performance are on the menu in this challenging but extremely rewarding (and often hilarious), courtroom exercise.

Divide the players into pairs, ask them to sit in a socially distanced space, and distribute a pen and piece of paper to each player. Next, ask each pair to decide who is to be the defence and who will be the prosecution. Explain that they are no longer drama students but high-powered lawyers who have been assigned to some of the most high-profile cases ever to come to court. Their task is to pit their wits against their fellow players and attempt to form the strongest argument in order to win the case.

The cases should be made up, based on famous works of fiction and fairy tales. You can either prepare some ideas before the start of the session, or ask each pair to invent their own. In each case, a character is facing charges for their 'crimes', such as:

★ The Big Bad Wolf accused of destroying a little pig's straw house.

★ Cinderella's Wicked Stepmother accused of child neglect.

★ Jack (of the Beanstalk) accused of destroying property and murder.

★ The Wolf (from *Red Riding Hood*) accused of eating an OAP.

★ Goldilocks accused of porridge theft.

★ Dorothy (just arrived in Oz) accused of witch murder.

The two lawyers will each have thirty seconds to convince the jury (the audience) of the guilt or innocence of the accused. Since these cases are all based on works of fiction, the cases can also be packed full of as much 'fiction' as the defence/prosecution lawyers can conjure up! Flair is more important than fact here – and the lawyers must concoct whatever story they can to prove, beyond any reasonable doubt, that their client is innocent or guilty. Allow ten minutes for the lawyers to prepare their cases as you set up the courtroom (a couple of socially distanced tables and chairs ought to do it).

With preparation time over, invite one pair to take to the courtroom in the case of the Court versus Voldemort (or whichever character). Toss a coin to see which lawyer will go first and let the arguments commence! In performance, players must use all their powers of persuasion to convince the audience of their case. They must show confidence, determination, truth, passion, focus – whilst using eye contact and charisma to attempt to connect with the jury.

Once both arguments have been made, it's time for the verdict, so ask the audience for a show of hands to decide if the accused is 'Guilty' or 'Not Guilty'. Then it's on to the next case...

# 44

# 3-Call Love Story

Character, truth and connection are explored in this simple but highly immersive exercise about interpersonal relationships.

Ask the group to pair up and ask all players to have their mobile phones with them (ensuring, of course, that they are turned off!). When phones have been retrieved, explain that each pair are a long-standing couple who have been together for many, many years, and that the aim of this exercise is to give a snapshot of their relationship in just three telephone calls, each lasting thirty seconds.

As we know, all good stories have a beginning, a middle and an end... and that is just what we will explore here: the start of the relationship, a significant moment during the relationship, and finally, sadly, the end!

Choices, as ever, are all important here. Each phone call must pack a powerful punch, from the flushes of young love, via a significant moment midway through the relationship, to the dramatic final conversation. Players should try to cram as much into these ninety seconds of dialogue as possible, but the overall length of the relationship can be up to the pair. There may well have been forty, fifty, sixty years between the first and last conversations, so this should be reflected in the vocal quality and tone of each successive conversation.

As you send the players away to work on the content of their three conversations, you should prepare the playing area for the performance. This will be, very simply, two chairs positioned some distance apart, allowing for an audience in the round. You should also cue up your sound effects for the exercise: a simple phone ring will do it, but I like to go the extra mile and provide a ticking-clock sound effect culminating in a phone ring to signify the passage of time. I also find that this longer sound effect allows players a few additional, vital moments to prepare for the conversation to come.

Once rehearsal time is up, ask the players to form an audience and have each couple enter the playing area, in turn, to tell the story of their relationship in just three brief phone conversations. If players have made strong choices it's all about committing once the performance begins and building up that fourth wall through which the audience view the relationship. For those who dare to commit and connect to their partner, the rewards will be obvious – and some very fulfilling work can be achieved from this simple but highly creative exercise.

# Cyber-Bully

**This high-impact exercise asks players to explore the difficult subject of cyber-bullying, and to lay bare its dangers in a hard-hitting infomercial.**

As this Main Course deals with such a challenging subject – one which some of your group may have personal experience of – it's essential to create a safe space and offer some supportive information about bullying online and on social media. Use gathered facts as the basis of a discussion about the prevalence and impact of cyber-bullying, such as:

★ About 37% of young people between the ages of twelve and seventeen have been bullied online. 30% have had it happen more than once.

★ About half of LGBTQ+ students experience online harassment – a rate higher than average.

★ Young people who experience cyber-bullying are at a greater risk than those who don't for both self-harm and suicidal behaviours.

★ 83% of young people believe social-media companies should be doing more to tackle cyber-bullying on their platforms.

★ 60% of young people have witnessed online bullying. Most do not intervene.

★ Only one in ten teen victims will inform a parent or trusted adult of their abuse.

*Source: do something.org*

After the discussion, divide the players into groups of three and ask that they devise an online infomercial of no longer than thirty seconds that packs a powerful punch and warns of the dangers of cyber-bullying. Creative thinking is to be encouraged here... tearing up the rulebook and entering the world of the abstract is very much to be applauded and encouraged, especially if it gets the message across in a memorable way.

The devising should (of course) be done at a safe distance, so it's a good idea to suggest that the cyber-bully is placed in a fixed position on one side of the stage, the victim of the abuse similarly fixed on the opposite side of the stage, leaving the third player free to move between them whilst observing social distance. Beyond that, the players should feel free to construct their piece in whatever way they see fit, but it needs to grab the attention of the audience instantly and leave a lasting impression.

With parameters of the task set, allocate twenty minutes for groups to create a game-changing, powerful anti-cyber-bullying campaign. When the time comes to share their infomercials, you will often be stunned by the creativity, ingenuity and passion on display, with some highly impactful work created from this premise.

# 46 Tales of the Unexpected

This creative exercise requires close connection between performers and a strong focus in performance.

Ask players to pair up, to find a suitably distanced space and to sit whilst you explain the exercise. Next, place two chairs side by side in the playing area and explain that this two-chair set-up is actually a motor vehicle.

Each pair is to devise a performance piece that starts with one player driving a car/van/lorry. As they're driving along, the second player should walk into the road causing the vehicle to skid to a halt. When the driver exits the car, seething with anger at the careless pedestrian's actions, it will quickly dawn on them that something otherworldly is happening. The person in the road is not merely a careless pedestrian – something much more 'unexpected' is afoot here...

So, who is this careless pedestrian? Well, that is completely down to the players' imaginations and they should be encouraged to think creatively. It could be that the driver's daughter, who passed away last spring, has risen from the grave... or the driver is from the future and has come with a warning of impending doom... or the ghost of a person killed by the driver is here to get revenge... The more daring and creative their choices are, the more powerful and engaging the unfolding drama will be. Players should ensure that there is a definite reason for the character/spectre/creature to be there. This is not a chance meeting; they have tracked the driver down for a reason and that reason will be revealed in the scene.

This exercise makes it particularly easy to maintain distance because, with such an unexpected visitor, the terrified driver will very much want to remain a car's length away! Players should build the narrative up to a dramatic conclusion and, if you have access to theatre lighting, it can be employed particularly effectively here. Keep the lighting dim throughout and ask for the players to give you a cue for either a slow fade to black or snap blackout (depending on the nature of the dramatic finale).

In performance, it's always exciting and entertaining for the audience to watch these 'tales of the unexpected', since no one knows what they're going to get! Players must bring total commitment and focus to the playing area and dare to immerse themselves in the created world, producing some wonderfully surprising and original work as a result.

# The News

**This fun exercise, suitable for younger players, encourages clear staging, strong teamwork and engaging character playing.**

In this exercise, the players will become crack news teams, breaking the latest big stories, so before the session you should prepare a number of stories that will make the headlines in tonight's bulletin. As this is a slightly eccentric version of the news, these headlines should be suitably wacky (and offer good scope for character playing), such as:

★ Talking Dog Plans World Domination!

★ Robot Teacher on the Rampage!

★ World's Smallest Person Found in Crisp Packet!

The more ridiculous the better! Armed with your headlines, it's time to prepare the studio. This exercise works particularly well when keeping players at a distance is a priority, as all participants are, by the very nature of the piece, located in separate areas. There should be a news desk on one side of the playing area, and the interviews can be placed at least two metres away from the studio.

Divide the players into groups of three and ask them to find a space whilst you navigate the room, distributing three headlines to each group. With headlines distributed, instruct each group to produce a news programme, using only the given headlines as their stimulus. When the programme begins, the newsreader will read out the first headline, giving a general overview of the story, before handing over to a colleague who will have tracked down a central character in the story to interview: the talking dog, the robot teacher, the crisp eater, or whatever weird and wonderful character the story calls for! The interviewee has the most challenging role here, as they must play three contrasting and dynamic characters – encourage them to bring as much colour and contrast as they can to these characterisations so that each one is distinctly and dramatically different.

This setting works very well as the players don't need to worry about staging or getting too close; they can focus on the content and the character. It's a good idea to play a sound effect or jingle between each headline so that players can switch position/roles, allowing each performer to play the newsreader, the interviewer and the interviewee.

If working in an online setting, this exercise can be played in two ways... *Improvised*: Select the news anchor, interviewer and interviewee before typing a news headline into the chat box and letting the off-the-cuff news report play out! *Structured*: Divide the players into small groups, allocate three headlines per group, and have them rehearse their news programmes in breakout rooms. Both versions work equally well and it just depends on the time you have available and the maturity of the players as to which option works best for you and your group.

*Main Courses*

# Mask My Movements

**An exercise to help less experienced performers orient themselves in the playing area (and as a bonus, it helps to keep players at a distance).**

Main Courses

Young or inexperienced performers can often take time to master the art of intelligent, intuitive staging. This exercise speeds up the process by pinpointing exactly where they should position their bodies.

Begin by dividing the players into groups of three and asking that they devise a short piece using a title you provide (for example, *The Bully*, *The Hunt for Blackbeard's Treasure* or *The Revenge of the Evil Headmaster*). Before they can get to work, it's time to mask their movements! Ask that they form an audience whilst you position yourself in the centre of the playing area, clutching a roll of masking tape and a pen. Reassure them that you're not about to give a lecture on home improvements – rather, you're going to mark out the stage positions that they will take up in their performance piece.

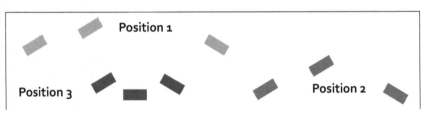

Start by tearing off three pieces of tape and placing them in suitably spaced, upstage positions, and writing the number '1' on them. These mark the three players' opening positions in the scene; players should stand on a piece of tape each, ensuring that both feet are placed firmly on the tape, positioning them at an appropriate angle. Next, mark out Position 2 and finally Position 3 (with the central piece of tape in Position 3, ask that the performer places their knees on it as opposed to their feet). In an instant, you have marked out a series of stage positions and directions that will keep the performers distanced, working in suitable areas of the stage, and angled towards the audience at all times. All they have to do now is work out a storyline that fits the marked-out stage positions.

In performance, the players will find it easier to hit intelligent positions and the created work will be all the more watchable for it. It's a good idea to repeat this exercise in future sessions, using new positions and different titles each time, as it's amazing how quickly this way of working gets into the muscle-memory of the performers. Before long, they will be making inventive staging choices of their own without being tied to the tape.

# Theatre in the Dark

**This exercise encourages even the most reserved performer to 'let go' fully in the playing area, whilst keeping distance in performance.**

Divide the players into pairs and set a title for the performance piece to come; for the purpose of this exercise, a title with scope for emotional depth works best, something like *The End* would offer ample opportunity for strong, emotion-fuelled work (but you are, of course, free to choose your own!). With title set, ask the players to devise the background to the narrative... What is coming to an end? Why is it coming to an end? How do they feel about this demise? The more information they have, the deeper they will be able to immerse themselves in the created world, so players should be as thorough as possible in their preparations. This is a rather unique exercise because there is no real need to rehearse the performance aspect of the work; the most important part of the preparation is the gathering of information, as well as ensuring that both players are on the same page.

Once all pairs have decided upon a suitable scenario, allocated roles and discussed their feelings towards the imminent 'end', instruct the players to form an audience in the round and place two distanced chairs in the playing area. Now, invite one pair to sit on the chairs and explain that they are to act out their scene from these sitting positions, but – and here comes the twist – the audience will not be able to see them as they perform because they will be acting in the dark. Before you dim the lights, instruct the performers to allow a moment or two for the darkness to fully descend and for them to become fully focused before they speak... So, slowly fade the lights to black (or flick the light switch off) and wait for the drama to unfold!

Even without visual connection with the other, some incredibly engaging, electric theatre can be produced, and you will often be amazed at the power of the performances that can come soaring through the darkness. When the scene has come to an end, allow a moment for the audience (and players) to digest what has just transpired, before turning the lights back on. After allowing a beat to acclimatise to the light, ask the performers how it felt to perform in such conditions. The universal answer will be that they felt much more able to let go, fully inhabit their character and connect with the emotion of the piece, without feeling the pressure of the audience glaring at them.

Repeat this process with all pairs and, by the end of the exercise, the players will feel that they have given something of themselves, which is always a fantastic achievement and one that should be celebrated. Following the exercise, players should be encouraged to bring the same courage and conviction when they are next in the full glare of the lights.

# 50

# 3-Pic Play

**This highly creative exercise encourages players to bring control and clarity to their acting work.**

Divide the players into pairs and ask all pairs (except one) to form an audience seated in the round. Invite the standing pair into the playing area, and instruct them to form a tableau by showing them what to do and asking them to copy you (or getting suggestions from the audience) – for instance, one player in Superman pose, flexing muscles, and the other kneeling in prayer position.

Ask all players to note this as Tableau 1. Now, it's time to rearrange the scene – so reform the players into all new positions of your choosing. Players should note that this is Tableau 2. And finally – I think you've got where we're going with this now! – rearrange the players into an all-new dynamic and suitably distanced still image, Tableau 3.

Now, ask each pair to create a short performance piece that incorporates the three tableaux into a piece of theatre. They must hit the three positions in the order in which they were demonstrated and, most importantly, they must be as accurate as possible with their body positions. Each time the narrative arrives at one of the given images, they should freeze for a brief moment (to note the tableau) before the action moves on... The scene will end on the final tableau, which should be held into blackout (if possible). Ask that the narrative moves naturally from one position to the next; players shouldn't just throw themselves into the given positions, they must organically arrive at each set position. Ask, too, that they remain suitably distanced for the duration of the scene.

Allocate a period of time for rehearsals and let the 3-Pic Play devising begin. Circulate the room (or rooms if possible) and coach players not only to bring energy but also control to their work, so that each tableau is created with precision and care. When rehearsals are over, ask that players form an audience and watch each group, in turn, perform their 3-Pic Plays. Following each performance, discuss whether the players had hit the exact position of each tableau. This is harder than it seems, especially in the heat of performance, but hitting their marks and keeping to agreed blocking are key skills for performers to master. With focus, clear thinking and a strong awareness of others, the group will develop and improve over time. Try increasing the number and complexity of the tableaux into 4-, 5- or even 6-Pic Plays!

# Motivation Maps

**Bringing control to the playing area and learning how to follow marked stage directions is developed in this physically engaging exercise.**

Using Motivation Maps is a great way of helping inexperienced performers get to grips with their 'place of work' (the stage!) – and, as an additional bonus, they are a useful tool for keeping performers safely distanced in performance. Before the session, you should prepare a number of Motivation Maps, which consist of several sheets of paper, mapping out the stage directions of each performer within a scene, such as the following:

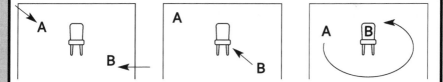

About five sheets of simple stage directions should be about right; it's a good idea to prepare a Motivation Map for a group of three as well, just in case you are faced with an odd number of players.

Next, divide the players into pairs, distribute the maps and instruct them to prepare a scene that precisely follows the mapped-out stage directions. Here comes the motivation bit: there has to be a clear and definite reason for moving from one area of the stage to another. Players should never cross the stage simply because the map tells them to do so; their movements must be driven by a strong impulse. Discourage players from making any additional movements beyond those that are mapped out for them, and encourage each movement to be clear and purposeful.

This exercise encourages players to connect physical movement with emotion and motivation, bringing a greater sense of spatial awareness to their work. It is also particularly useful to demonstrate how dramatic staging can be noted in performers' scripts, a skill that should be utilised in future productions.

Main Courses

# The Scottish Play

Few openings are as dramatic and atmospheric as Shakespeare's great work and, even socially distanced, it still has the power to ignite endless creativity.

Divide the players into groups of three, before allocating each player with their dramatic, other-worldly scripts from the opening of (whisper it!) *Macbeth*:

| | |
|---|---|
| FIRST WITCH. | When shall we three meet again<br>In thunder, lightning, or in rain? |
| SECOND WITCH. | When the hurlyburly's done,<br>When the battle's lost and won. |
| THIRD WITCH. | That will be ere the set of sun. |
| FIRST WITCH. | Where the place? |
| SECOND WITCH. | Upon the heath. |
| THIRD WITCH. | There to meet with Macbeth. |
| FIRST WITCH. | I come, Graymalkin! |
| SECOND WITCH. | Paddock calls. |
| THIRD WITCH. | Anon. |
| ALL. | Fair is foul, and foul is fair:<br>Hover through the fog and filthy air. |

With scripts distributed, challenge the players to produce as dynamic and creative an interpretation of this classic dialogue as possible, whilst at all times adhering to the rules of social distance. Encourage the use of physical and vocal levels, dynamic characterisation, vocal effects (such as cannon or echo, etc.), sound effects, dramatic lighting... anything that they have at their disposal that will enable them to create as atmospheric a piece as possible.

This exercise works extremely well with the audience in the round as it creates an enclosed and focused space with maximum playing area for the performers to explore. The power that Shakespeare's great play has, even to this day, is astonishing, as well as its ability to inspire creativity from performers of all ages. This exercise rarely fails to produce interesting, focused and highly creative work.

# The Final Goodbye

**An exercise to bring truth, focus, connection and commitment into the playing area.**

This simple premise can be the catalyst for some very stimulating and – although physically distanced – highly connected work. Ask the players to pair up and then to form an audience in the round, whilst you place two tables and chairs in the playing area as follows (two tables ensures players stay at a safe distance):

So, what is to transpire either side of this table? Well, as the title suggests, it will be an emotional and final goodbye... Explain that there will be a player sat either side of the table. Firstly, they must decide *where* they are, *who* they are and *why* they will never see each other again. Choices should be as strong and dramatic as possible, like the following examples:

★ A parent going to visit their condemned child in prison for the final time.

★ A girl stands on the deck of a ship, bound for a new life in Australia. Her best friend bids a tearful goodbye from the quayside.

★ A child being separated from their mother at a concentration camp.

★ Two people clinging onto a life raft before one gives up (chairs would obviously be dispensed with here).

★ An ill patient saying goodbye to a family member.

★ A father saying goodbye to his son at a border crossing.

★ Two dancers say goodbye (from either side of a glitter ball) after being voted off a dance competition.

Strong choices are important if this is to be an emotional and engaging goodbye. Saying goodbye to a colleague who you've worked with for five weeks isn't likely to provide sufficiently high stakes or lead to very powerful drama. Players should be encouraged to take risks and dare to conceive scenarios that will challenge them and demand that they give emotionally of themselves.

If players have the courage to take risks and throw themselves head-first into an emotional scenario, some very compelling work will be created from this premise.

# Generation Script

Strong characterisations are explored as players must depict several generations through scripted dialogue.

Main Courses

For this generation-spanning exercise, you will need to prepare a handful of Generation Scripts featuring several characters of totally different generations. The Dickens-inspired script below works particularly well as it depicts a young caroller (or carollers), middle-aged Bob Cratchit, old Scrooge and, finally, the deceased Marley. That's quite a mix – and it also offers good scope for social distancing as these are not characters that would want to get up close to one another!

SCROOGE. Close the door, Cratchit! There's a draught as cold as Christmas!

CRATCHIT. Right away, sir.

*Before he can close the door, a* CAROLLER *appears.*

CAROLLER. Penny or a farthing, sir?

CRATCHIT. I think you would be wise to try somewhere else.

CAROLLER. Ain't no law against it!

CRATCHIT. I beg you... Move on!

SCROOGE. Why is the door still open, Cratchit?!

CAROLLER. Penny or a farthing, sir?

SCROOGE. What did you say?!...

CAROLLER. Christmas charity, sir?

SCROOGE. Charity?

CAROLLER. Yeah, you know... Christmas? Good will to all men?

SCROOGE. I would rather burn every pound note I possess than give to charity! Now, get away!

CAROLLER. But, sir?!

SCROOGE. I said GO!

CONTINUED...

SCROOGE *slams the door on the* CAROLLER.

Well? Get to work, Cratchit!

CRATCHIT. But... it's Christmas evening, sir.

SCROOGE. And, no doubt, you'll be wanting tomorrow off too?!

CRATCHIT. If it's quite convenient, sir.

SCROOGE. It is not! But go now, before I change my mind!

CRATCHIT. Yes, sir. Merry Christmas, sir.

CRATCHIT *exits hurriedly.*

SCROOGE. Christmas?! Bah humbug!!

*Silence, then there is a rattle at the door.*

I told you... No charity!

MARLEY. I come not for charity, Ebenezer Scrooge!

SCROOGE. Agghhh! Be gone, foul spirit!

MARLEY. Foul indeed! The foulest to have haunted the earth! But not as foul as you will become!

SCROOGE. What do you want with me?

MARLEY. To warn you! I am your future, Ebenezer!

SCROOGE. That can't be!

MARLEY. It will be! Unless you change it. You will be visited by three ghosts tonight. Heed their words! Only then can you change your destiny!

MARLEY *exits.* SCROOGE *is left in a state of shock.*

The challenge is for the performers to vary the vocal delivery and physical characteristics of each character so that the contrasting ages are very clearly represented in the playing. This is quite a task, but it's a great way of encouraging players to unlock the potential of the script. They will see how an array of dynamic and contracting characterisations can be drawn from one simple scene if they are prepared to push the boundaries and dare to bring diversity to the stage. Have fun creating your own scripts!

*Note: If playing online, players should be encouraged to stay relatively close to the screen and to make full use of vocal dynamism and facial expression whilst portraying the various characters. Performances can become a little lost if they wander too far from the screen so they should prepare for their close-up and fill the screen with as much focus, colour and contrast of character as possible.*

# Set Chairs

> This Main Course encourages performers to bring control to the playing
> area and to work in intelligent, watchable areas of the stage.

Young or inexperienced performers can sometimes struggle to anchor their
stage work, becoming so immersed in the created world that they forget all
about the watching audience and end up performing in areas of the stage that
make it impossible for the audience to engage with or even to see the action...
Cue the Set Chairs exercise!

First of all, allocate players into groups of three and ask them to form a socially
distanced audience whilst you position a number of chairs in the playing area.
Something like this will work:

Announce that the title of their performance piece will be *The Trip to Disaster!*
The three chairs downstage are to be the mode of transport used to go on the
trip (this can be a bus, a train, a rocket ship, a giant elephant... anything at all!),
and the angled chairs stage-left constitute the destination that they are
travelling to. The players must either sit or stand on these chairs until disaster
strikes and they can either make a dash for it (back to the mode of transport) or
the lights can simply fade to black.

What you will find in the playing is that the chairs help to anchor the work and
keep players working in good, watchable areas of the stage, staying suitably
distanced from each other. This is such an effective device for encouraging
clarity and control in performance and, after several Set Chairs scenes have
been played out – with different positioning of chairs and different scene titles
– players will become accustomed to working at specific angles and in certain
areas of the stage. As a result, more considered use of the playing area will be
seen in future performances.

# Another Level

Shakespeare's famous love story came from famously socially distanced beginnings so, if socially distanced drama is good enough for Romeo and Juliet... it's good enough for us!

Divide the players into pairs and explain that each pair is to recreate a Shakespearean balcony scene. But... this recreation will not quite be in the image of the Bard's great masterpiece because, with a bit of creativity and some outside-the-box thinking, the classic balcony scene is to be reimagined.

Pairs should decide between them who is to be the elevated object of affection and who will be stuck at ground level attempting to curry favour with a high-rise hottie! Unlike Romeo and Juliet, in this scene, the wooer must work incredibly hard to win the heart of the object of their affection, who initially should spurn their advances. Creative thinking is to be encouraged here when deciding how it is that the wooer finally manages to win the affection of their heart's desire.

Players should feel free to set the scene wherever they like – it could be in fair Verona, but similarly it could be at the foot of a castle turret with a handsome prince attempting to win over a fair maiden (or vice versa), or outside a council flat where a teenager tries to impress his or her school crush... As long as one player is raised high and the other on ground level then the sky is (quite literally) the limit!

A well-placed table or chair should be fine for standing on, but ensure that they are suitably sturdy and that the elevated players are comfortable whilst standing up there, looking down on their wooer.

This premise never fails to ignite creativity, and players universally love the challenge of bagging their turret-bound sweetheart. And after many variations and mutations of the balcony scene have been performed, you will never watch *Romeo and Juliet* in quite the same light again!

## Variation: Life on the Ledge

Once the love stories have played out, ask the players to switch levels (those who were previously elevated should return to ground level and vice versa) and introduce a completely different dynamic to the multi-level play. This time, it's all about 'life on the ledge' – the elevated player is on the brink of despair and the ground-level player must attempt to talk them down from the ledge. Players must be very clear about who they are and why things have come to this point of drastic action. At the end of the emotional encounter, players should choose from a slow fade or snap blackout.

# The Object of the Exercise

A wacky but rewarding exercise that breathes life into the simplest of household objects.

Main CourSeS

Before the session, you should source several objects. It's a good idea to get groupings of objects from specific rooms – for instance, a pepper grinder, a salt cellar, a spatula, a rolling pin and a toothpick from the kitchen. Try to pick a collection of objects that vary in size, as this will make for more interesting and dynamic work.

Ask the players to sit in a socially distanced audience, and request four volunteers to sit two metres apart in front of the playing area. You are to 'cast' them in the forthcoming presentation, so let's say Player 1 is the salt cellar, Player 2 is the pepper grinder, Player 3 is the spatula, and Player 4 is the toothpick. Now, it's time to bring the stars of the show into the playing area, so place the objects – the pepper grinder and salt cellar – next to each other and ask that the corresponding players start to voice a conversation between these two 'characters'. Players should consider the size, shape and function of the object when deciding upon the voice and personality of their character, and make them as varied as possible. After a short while, bring the spatula into the action and then the toothpick (and if you need to add a final character into the mix, you always have the rolling pin!). After the action has run its course, and hilarity has been had, bring the improvisation to a close, choose four new players, four new objects and start over.

Try this improvised version of the exercise several times before bringing more structure to the play. Divide the players into groups of three or four, and ask each person to choose an object each. They must now prepare a scene between their objects that lasts for one minute and contains a dramatic revelation. Allow the players twenty minutes or so to work out their plot and rehearse before presenting their scene.

It's amazing how effective this exercise can be, and what a rich collage of characters are on display. For some performers, taking away the pressure of physically being on stage allows them to bring much more freedom and vibrancy to their character work. Although seemingly ridiculous, it can encourage a level of dynamism in performance that you will not quite have believed possible!

This exercise works particularly effectively in an online setting – rather than having actual objects, you can just source images of objects and use the screen-share facility to show those images to the participants. Be sure to ask everyone, apart from the chosen performers, to mute their microphones before the action commences and encourage players to listen closely to their fellow performers before making their own contribution.

*Note: You may want to ask players to bring their own objects in from home, to avoid different individuals touching the same objects and having to sanitise them between rounds.*

# Contrast

**Creative writing, sustained focus and truth are all skills advanced in this challenging exercise.**

Divide the players into pairs and ask them to find a socially distanced space in which to work. Next, distribute paper and pens and ask that every player writes a fictitious monologue of no longer than one minute and written in the first person (using 'I...'), which is inspired by a title of your choice. The chosen title should offer a myriad of creative possibilities, so something like:

★ *Prom-Night Memories*

★ *Holiday Romance*

★ *The Office Party*

★ *Remembering Father*

These open titles work well as one person's experience of a holiday romance, office party or whatever can differ vastly from the next. One player's prom night might end with them falling in love, whilst another's concludes with a terrible ordeal that scars them for life. Although every player's monologue is inspired by the same stimulus, what you're aiming at is work that demonstrates a high degree of contrast.

In performance, it will not be a case of Player 1 reading their monologue to be followed by Player 2 reading theirs... Monologues should be divided into at least three sections, and then intertwined, with one player reading a section and then pausing as the other speaks, and back again, with the focus shifting between the two players. Players should consider carefully when to switch between narratives, so that they offer the optimum impact and contrast; they might even decide to speak some lines at the same time if this adds to the overall dramatic impact of the piece.

When it comes to performing the short piece, have one player position themselves stage-right and the other stage-left. Use lighting (if possible) to set the mood and let the see-saw of contrasting emotions play out. The important thing is that players remain focused and 'in the moment' when not speaking so that, when they pick up the baton, they are still in the same place emotionally and able to bring a consistency to their performance.

It's a challenging exercise, but when it all comes together, some extremely powerful work can be created – and, of course, there are many full plays that are constructed from interwoven monologues in just this way.

*Note: Breakout rooms will need to be used for this exercise to work in an online setting.*

# 59    Set Positions

**This exercise is excellent for inspiring creativity and encouraging players to bring control and structure to their dramatic work.**

Divide the players into pairs and ask them to form a socially distanced audience whilst you explain the exercise. Place a table and two chairs in the playing area, lay a piece of paper on the table and ask players to note that this is Position 1.

Now rearrange the furniture... place one of the chairs on its side, rip up the piece of paper and throw it on the floor, and ask the players to note that this is Position 2. Obviously these positions and props can be wherever and whatever you want them to be, but you should consider the ability to remain distanced whilst choosing your set-up.

Each pair must now prepare a scene that starts with the furniture/props in Position 1 and ends with them in Position 2. Encourage them to be as creative as possible with the series of dramatic events that leads to this rearrangement, and explain that there must be a very definite reason for the chair to be pushed onto its side and the paper to be ripped, and so on.

Because the parameters are very clear, players tend to revel in this exercise and are rarely stuck for ideas or inspiration. They have a definite idea of where the scene is headed and, as a result, their ideas become much more structured and focused. Knowing the endgame brings drive and clarity of focus to an actor's work with strong, dynamic performances.

# Greek Chorus

**Passion, commitment, creativity, emotional connection and teamwork are all on the agenda in this engaging exercise for older players.**

Greek tragedy still very much has a place in the modern drama class, with its unrivalled power to engage and enthuse, and players revelling in its passion and scale. Abiding by social distancing, but not losing the raw passion of performance, can be achieved by letting the Greeks come to the rescue! The Greek chorus is an excellent solution to the potential predicament of socially distanced dramatic work; any action that can't physically be shown can be narrated by the chorus, leaving the players safe, and the audience informed and engaged throughout.

It's a good idea to start your Greek odyssey with some scripted work – and in the Resource Pack is a three-part script inspired by the Orpheus myth, but you can also write your own. Divide the players into groups of five, which will allow for a small (but mighty) Greek chorus of three, and allocate them one of the scripts (hopefully you'll have enough performers for all three parts to be performed). The players should be as creative as possible with the way that they use the chorus: different levels (both vocal and physical), use of cannon (both vocal and physical), unified/synchronised movement and stylised choreography, vocalised emotional outpouring... It's a good idea to allow players to go a little 'off-script' if they wish, adding additional words, sounds or dialogue – but only if they feel that it will significantly enhance the piece.

Players should ensure that they remain socially distanced at all times, but despite the distance they must strive to remain connected to one other and to the tale being told... If they succeed in doing this, then some incredibly impactful and powerful work can be produced.

Following the scripted performance, ask players to remain in their groups and to produce a second piece, which should be a devised modern take on Greek tragedy. Keep with similar themes (doomed love, in the case of Orpheus) – but this must be brought right up to date, set in the modern day, whilst still employing a traditional Greek chorus. This task never fails to ignite creativity of the players, who will revel in the unorthodox challenge and often return with some highly original and engaging work.

# Desserts

In this edition of *Drama Menu*, the Dessert course features a collection of games and exercises that work well in an online setting, and they have all been tried and tested during drama sessions on Zoom. So, start up your video-conferencing software, and unleash the creative-learning potential of the online world.

You will also find most of them can be conducted in person as well – though make sure players keep socially distanced at all times, of course.

# Puncture Walk

**A technical exercise that helps develop breath control and vocal power.**

Ask the players to find a space and to lie on their backs with knees up. Once lying comfortably, instruct that they breathe in through the nose on a count of four – and then out through the mouth on a count of eight. The breath should be released with a 'sssssss' sound, like a deflating tyre... or a snake... or hissing at the baddie in a panto... you get the idea! Repeat this, three or four times, reciting the mantra: 'Breathing in, two, three, four – and out, two, three, four, five, six, seven, eight.' After the players have successfully navigated eight counts with a continuous and consistent 'sssssss' sound, raise the stakes and breathe out on a count of sixteen, then thirty-two, and if you're feeling very adventurous, go for sixty-four! Players should focus on breathing into the lower back, so that the breath is deep, the diaphragm is engaged and the hissing sound is consistent and controlled.

Now it's time to get the exercise on its feet (as players will rarely be flat on their backs for the duration of a performance). Ask everyone to stand, and then explain to them that they are about to take a deep breath in on a count of four as before, only this time, as they start to exhale on a 'sssssss' sound, they should walk around their room (using whatever space they have available) and continue to walk until they can hiss no more. Once they have run out of breath, instruct the players to come to a standstill and sit down on the floor or return to their computer screen. The last player walking and exhaling is the winner.

It's a good idea to time this exercise and make a note of when the last player stopped walking... you can use this information in future sessions to gauge how the breathing capacity of the group is improving. With continued use, you should find that exhalation/walking time will be significantly increased.

*Note: Before you start the walking, discourage players from taking sneaky, mid-walk breaths. Such skulduggery is hard to spot online, so ask that players are honest and resist the urge to cheat!*

# Shake and Stretch

There is nothing more satisfying than a good, old-fashioned stretch – and this exercise is a great way of getting the players actively involved in an online session.

Let's start with a shake-out, so instruct all players to attempt to throw their right hands clean away from their bodies! After ten seconds or so of thrusting, throwing and shaking, change the focus to the left hand, so drop the right hand and attempt to launch left hands into the distance! After a further ten seconds, change the focus to the right foot and then the left foot – and for the grand finale, instruct all players to shake out both their hands and feet at the same time. On this final instruction, the entire screen (or room) will be thrown into a frantic, physical fling-fest until you bring the shake-out to a close!

With the warm-up process in full flow, it's now time for a stretch. Instruct the players to reach both their hands to the sky, imagining that there is a piece of string connected to every single fingertip, pulling them skywards. As the imaginary strings draw them up and they can reach no higher with their splayed fingers, instruct that they rise onto their tiptoes in order to stretch that extra couple of inches. Once all toes are tipped and fingers are straining for the sky, have them hold this position for a count of five. Get close to the screen here and if you see any players not fully committed to reaching every fingertip skywards, point out the non-stretching culprits and restart the countdown. Do this as many times as it takes for all players to join in!

So, begin the countdown: 'Five, four, three, two, one'... Then it's time to cut the imaginary cords and when you do, all players must collapse the upper half of their bodies, bending at the waist, so that their feet are firmly planted but their hands are touching the floor. Whilst in this position, ask the players to shake out their shoulders gently, before curling up through the spine on a count of eight. Once fully upright, it's time to repeat the process, so reattach the imaginary strings, get those feet on tiptoes, and send those fingers straining for the sky. This time, once in the collapsed position, rather than shaking out, ask the players to rock gently from side to side, gradually increasing the size of the swing before returning to the centre and curling up the spine as before.

This exercise can be used to warm up at the start of a session, getting the group engaged and energised, or as a warm-down at the end, like an athlete stretching the body out and returning to daily life.

Desserts

# 63 Ha-Ha-He-He-Ho-Ho-HUH!

A warm-up that encourages players to explore the full range of their vocal power.

Before the session, write the following words in large, clear letters on a piece of paper:

**Ha-Ha**

**He-He**

**Ho-Ho**

**HUH!**

Ask the players to stand and recite the words written on the card – practise this a few times and, once they've got the hang of it, it's time to add some parameters... This time, they are to repeat the mantra over and over, starting with no noise at all and gradually building up to a fully connected and projected sound.

Take a collective breath in (over a count of four) and then 'say', with no noise at all, 'Ha-Ha-He-He-Ho-Ho-HUH'! Now take another breath in and repeat the mantra with minimal vocal connection; now again using a slight whisper; now with a little more vocal connection... and a little more... and even more... until the sound is almost fully connected... and finally, encourage the final recital to be fully connected and forward-placed. The final sound should soar from the performers and hit the far wall of their room with clarity, volume and power!

This is an especially useful exercise to employ with groups of tentative, under-energised performers as it will prove that, with strong breath support and commitment, they have the vocal range and power to send their voices right to the back row – and beyond!

# Focus Fingers

**64**

An exercise for focusing minds when group focus is drifting.

Desserts

When you feel the need for an injection of focus and concentration, simply face the screen and circle your right arm through the air with your index finger pointed...

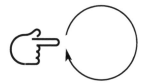

As you circle your arm, ask 'Who can do this?' This is usually enough to get the players intrigued and actively participating in the session (don't ask me why this is... but it works!). After a few rotations, the players will begin to wonder why they are participating in this mass circling. Before they have the chance to question it, hit them with the next part of the challenge. Ask them to drop their right arms, lift their left arms, point index fingers and start to draw a cross in the air.

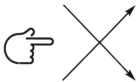

Once again, this challenge will be completed fairly easily, leaving the players wondering what this is all about. Well, they're about to find out!

Ask them to drop their left arm before shaking both arms out. Now, they should lift both arms and point both index fingers... here come the tricky bit! They are to attempt a right-handed circular motion and a left-handed cross at the same time. This is a lot harder than it seems and very few will be able to achieve it, but you will have achieved your goal of getting the group focused and ready for the next challenge. Very simple but very effective!

## 65

# What's My Job?

**This interactive mime exercise works very effectively as an online activity.**

Desserts

Before the session begins, you should get creative by writing as many job titles as you can think of on various slips of paper. These should be relatively simple and offer good scope for mime, such as:

★ Firefighter.

★ Chef.

★ Ice-cream seller.

★ Surgeon.

★ Farmer.

★ Croupier.

★ Lion tamer.

★ Swimming instructor.

★ Lumberjack.

Ensuring that you are in 'Gallery View', explain to the players that you are going to give them each a job title. You should start with the player at the top left and work your way around, and other players should close their eyes whilst each player is being given their job. Alternatively, you can use the chat function to write to each player individually.

After they have been awarded their 'job', each player will have ten seconds to jump up and mime it out. Declare who is going first – and as the player desperately fights an imaginary fire or operates on a burst appendix, all other players must write in the chat box what they think the job is. They only get one opportunity to guess, so they should be sure before they type. When the ten seconds are up, ask the miming player to read through the answers before revealing their job. Then choose the next player to start miming, and so on...

This is not always as straightforward as it seems, and players will quickly learn that they have to be extremely precise, committed and considered for their mime to be conveyed effectively to the watching audience.

Once all players have mimed their occupations, it's a good idea to have a second round in which the players decide for themselves what to mime – and why not change the subject (maybe hobbies)? Players whose jobs the audience failed to guess in the first round should work additionally hard the second time around to convey their mime effectively.

# 5 Seconds to Make

**This fun exercise requires physical creativity and quick thinking.**

Ask the players to walk around whatever space they have available to them, in the style of your choice: swimming, hopping, in slow motion, walking like they're on hot coals or through treacle... it's amazing how many possibilities there are when it comes to navigating a space.

Midway through the walking, call out 'freeze' and announce that they have five seconds to use their bodies to make an object: a banana, the Eiffel Tower, a piece of un-popped-up toast in a toaster, a beached whale... you get the idea; literally anything that your imagination can conjure! Repeat this two or three times, before having all players return to their screens.

Now, explain that there's going to be a competitive element to this second part of the exercise. The players will walk around, just as before, only this time, on your command of 'freeze', you will call out a letter and they have five seconds to morph their bodies into an animal starting with that letter.

So, call out 'D' and, once the five seconds are up, behold the weird and wonderful dogs, donkeys and duck-billed platypuses before you! It may be a good idea to ask every player to reveal their animal (as they won't always be completely obvious), and if two (or more) players have created the same animal, they are out and must sit down (or turn their screens off until the end of the exercise, so you can only see those still in play). If a player fails to think of an animal at all, they are also out. Continue this process until only one player remains, and declare them the winner.

This exercise works well as players quickly realise that going for the obvious will not see them triumph here; for success, they must use their imaginations and think outside the box. It's worth playing a further two or three rounds to see how much more original players become with their animal creation.

Desserts

# 67

# Yeah, and...

**A simple yet effective exercise that demonstrates the importance of listening, offering and accepting at the heart of all good improvisation.**

Players are going to have a conversation about something extraordinary that happened to them in the recent past... It shouldn't be something that actually happened but, for the purpose of this exercise, they should believe in the created truth. The conversation should begin with the words 'Do you remember when...'

It's a nice idea to ask the players to complete this opening offer by typing their ideas into the chat box. They may suggest – 'Do you remember when...'

'...we stole that go-kart?'

'...we got lost in the jungle?'

'...we kidnapped a celebrity chef?'

When the suggestions are in, choose your favourite and ask two players to begin a conversation, starting with the opening line and beyond that, every other line should start with the immortal words 'Yeah, and...', like the following:

'Do you remember when we kidnapped a celebrity chef?'

'Yeah, and... you told him to make a chocolate fondue.'

'Yeah, and... you ate it in one gulp.'

...and so it goes on, until the players run out of steam or you bring the exercise to a close.

This simple exercise demonstrates very effectively that players create good drama by accepting the ideas of others and offering their own. Ensure that each line starts with 'Yeah, and...', explaining that 'Yeah' is the acceptance, the 'and...' is the offering. Anything else – contradicting, saying no, or 'Yeah, but...' – blocks creativity and is unprogressive. By continually answering 'Yeah, and...', the story could technically go on forever, getting more and more extravagant. Encourage players to remain open to the possibilities, to keep listening proactively and working as closely as possible with their fellow performers, whilst resisting any urge to shut down the conversation or bring the tale to an end.

Choose another two players, take suggestions for a new story and start again. After each attempt, ask the audience: Did the players accept ideas and make progressive offers of their own? Did they/we believe in the story? Were the players sharing energy? Were they listening to one another? It's amazing how many skills can be drawn from such a simple exercise.

# Phone Reactions

**A simple yet effective exercise that encourages truth and focus in performance.**

Desserts

Ask the players to find their mobile phones – as they scurry around to find them, you should prepare the sound effect of a ringing phone.

Once players have returned and turned off their phones, explain that each of them is going to receive a phone call with some big news. What that news is will be decided by some adjectives that you have prepared earlier, and which should be as varied as possible:

| | | |
|---|---|---|
| EXCITING | SAD | CONFUSING |
| LIFE-CHANGING | FRUSTRATING | AMAZING |
| UNBELIEVABLE | DEVASTATING | HAPPY |

Ensuring that everyone is working in 'Gallery View', explain to the players that you are going to give them each an adjective. Start with the player in one corner of the screen and work your way around, and other players should close their eyes whilst each player is being given their word. Alternatively, you can use the chat function to write to each player individually before their turn.

The players must think of *what* the news is that they are about to receive and *why* it is so exciting/sad/demoralising, etc. Allow a few seconds for the players to make their choices before playing the phone sound effect. One by one, they are each to be given thirty seconds of time to engage in an imaginary conversation during which they receive the big news.

At the end of the exercise, ask the audience to guess what kind of news they believe the player received by typing it into the chat box. When all answers are in, the player can reveal the word they received. Players must be committed to successfully convey the emotion they're feeling; if they are not fully immersed in the truth of the phone call then it will be extremely tricky for the audience to guess the nature of the news. Continue until all players have participated.

Focus, listening and being 'in the moment' are all hugely important skills developed here; players should be encouraged to listen intently to what is being said on the phone and to react accordingly.

*Note: Ask all players to refrain from announcing the nature of the news during the call. If they blurt out 'This is such unbelievable/confusing/devastating news', it makes it a little too easy to guess!*

# 69

# Headline News

This quick-fire, quick-thinking game promotes listening, focus and creativity.

Ensuring that everyone is working in 'Gallery View', work round the 'room' numbering all participants from one. With numbers allocated, announce that they have all become newsreaders and it's a night of high drama in the newsroom! Explain that every time you call a number, the corresponding player must deliver a make-believe headline that makes sense and does not contain any pauses or hesitation. So, if you call out 'Five', that player may announce:

'Aliens seen above the White House. President calls it "Fake News".'

Then, 'Seven'...

'Eighty-year-old man breaks 100-metre-sprint record. Anti-doping officers are investigating.'

Now, 'Nine'...

'Uhhh...'

Freeze the exercise and eliminate Player 9 from the game (hesitation is banned)! Carry on until only one player remains, and declare them the winner.

This is a fun exercise to play but, through the fun, there are some important lessons to be learnt. Players must be prepared, they must be clear and concise whilst speaking, they must listen intently and, most importantly, they must demonstrate the ability to remain calm, collected and in control when put under pressure... not bad for a game about nonsense news!

As a variation, rather than reading the news headlines, players could be sports reporters, hosts of nature programmes or TV chefs inventing the names of elaborate dishes – but whatever genre you choose, the rules remain the same. Pause, hesitate, 'ummm' or 'errrr'... and you're out!

# Prop Play

A highly creative and enjoyable exercise that unleashes the actors' imaginations.

Allow exactly one minute for players to hunt around their houses and source an object of their choice – it can be anything at all, but ask that it is not too small, no smaller than a tennis ball, since tiny props don't come across to well on small screens. And... go!

Ensuring that everyone is working in 'Gallery View', work round the 'room' numbering all participants from one. With numbers allocated, ask all players to reveal their objects and, as they wave them around, explain that these objects are not what they think they are – in fact, they can be anything at all, other than what they see before them! By using the power of imagination, a simple frisbee can be transformed into a cereal bowl, a steering wheel, a saucepan, a hat... you get the idea. By letting their imaginations roam free, there is no limit to how many uses that frisbee can find!

To demonstrate the power of the actor's imagination, the players must transform their object into something completely different three times. Ask them to make sure that their transformations are visible and audible to all. We all want to hear the player say 'Mmmm, what delicious cereal' as they spoon cornflakes from the frisbee into their mouth or 'Caught one!' as they reel a fish in with their gold club! So, start the miming by calling out their numbers, and asking that player to demonstrate the all-new use for their object.

With the concept established and three rounds played, allocate a further minute to source a second object – and when they return, announce that now it's competition time! Divide the players into two teams and announce that players will pit their imaginations against each other. Choose one player from each team to go first (I like to type these names into the chat box in order to add to the drama) – these two players are now in focus and will participate in a 'Prop-off' to win a point for their team! Decide who's going first by tossing a coin and explain that each player has three seconds to invent a brand-new use for their object. Once started, they will take it in turns to demonstrate their weird and wonderful transforming objects until one player falters and fails to create a new use for the object within the given three seconds (or they repeat a use). At this point, the Prop-off is won by the other team, and they are awarded a point. Continue until all players have had a turn and declare the overall winning team.

By the end of all this game, players might be left with a slightly skewed sense of reality, but their imaginations will be well and truly alive and there should be a buzz of excitement surging through the group!

Desserts

# 71

# You're Late!

This mime exercise encourages teamwork, creativity and quick thinking.

Choose a player to play the role of a student arriving late for class (for older players, you can switch this scenario to an employee arriving late for work). Now, although the student is late, they don't know why... yet! It is the responsibility of all other players to help the latecomer discover the reason for their tardiness – and this will be done through the medium of mime!

Ask the student to close their eyes whilst you reveal the excuse for their lateness to everyone else. These excuses should be written on slips of paper and offer good scope for mime-play, such as:

★ Abducted by aliens.

★ Fell into a shark-infested water.

★ Met a celebrity.

★ Saved a dog from drowning.

Let's go with 'Abducted by aliens'. So, hold up the slip for all to see, and when you're happy that everyone has seen it and digested the information, hide the slip and ask the late student to open their eyes. They now have thirty seconds to guess why they are so late for school by watching as the players mime out the alien abduction scene. When thirty seconds are up, call 'Freeze', at which point all miming activity should immediately cease and the late student should reveal what they believe their excuse to be. Once they've made their guess, it's time to reveal the truth.

This exercise is trickier than it seems. With such an overload of gesturing and gurning focused towards one player, it's not always easy to make sense of it all. To succeed, mimes must be made as clear, succinct and specific as possible, whilst guessers must remain as relaxed and focused as they can, ignoring the pressure of the thirty-second countdown.

With the concept established, it's competition time! Divide the players into two teams. Choose the group to go first. They should decide who will play the late student and, once decided, the late student (and the other group) should close their eyes. With slip revealed, restart the timer and play as before. If the late student guesses correctly, they score a point for their team. If they fail to do so, their opponents have an opportunity to steal the point by guessing correctly. Continue this for five rounds – and then announce the winning team.

# The Object of History

A challenging storytelling exercise that encourages creative, outside-the-box thinking.

Allow one minute for players to search their houses or gardens for an object – it can be anything at all, but it's a good idea to declare a technology ban... So, less Mum's iPad and more a mug-tree from the kitchen. When the minute is up and all players have returned, ask them to hold aloft their objects... Brilliant, you're ready to begin!

Announce that today you're going on a field trip and will visit a museum that houses the most valuable collection of artifacts in the world! These artifacts are of huge historical importance and are all utterly priceless. The players are to take on the role of museum curators and, one at a time, they reveal an object of jaw-dropping interest and have thirty seconds to talk to the group about its significance.

They may describe how the mug-tree in their hand is, in fact, a jewellery holder, used by none other than Cleopatra to display all her favourite jewel-encrusted charms. They may go on to inform the group that this jewellery holder was found in her hand when she succumbed to the asp bite. It can be as far-fetched as possible whilst still retaining a modicum of plausibility!

With the premise established, work around all curators, one at a time, until they have all given an in-depth insight into their object. Players should be encouraged to provide as much information as possible about their chosen object and its origins, and to believe wholeheartedly in this created truth. If they believe it and deliver their talk with conviction, you may start to wonder if that teacup really was the reason we won the war or whether that chopping board was genuinely used to serve grapes to Caesar!

This is a fun exercise, but is also a very effective device for encouraging creative thinking and for honing the skill of remaining calm, considered and eloquent under pressure.

**73**

# Movie Mime

This physical mime exercise is a useful way to involve all players actively in the session.

Number the players and ask them to think about their favourite movie... but don't explain why just yet. With favourite movies at the forefront of their minds, announce to Player 1 that they have thirty seconds to demonstrate what movie is in their mind through the medium of mime.

Start the timer and, when the time is up, ask all players to guess the movie by typing in the chat box (it's a good idea to have everyone reveal their answers at the same time, which prevents people from copying others' answers). With guesses made, Player 1 should reveal their movie title. Players will often be surprised at just how much miming it takes to fill the thirty seconds, and how precise they have to be in order to convey the mime accurately. If they are anything other than fully committed and extremely clear then it can be quite confusing to those watching. With this in mind, have all other players mime out their chosen movies, with players guessing each time.

Once all players have mimed, it's competition time! Divide the players into two teams and ask the first team to choose a player to start. All other players should close their eyes whilst you show them a movie title. In this competitive round, players have just *fifteen* seconds to mime the movie title, which adds an extra element of urgency and excitement to the play. With the title allocated, the other players open their eyes and then you start the clock. When the fifteen seconds are up, give ten seconds for the team to type their answers into the chat box. If any of them are right, they score a point; if wrong, it's over to their opponents, who have ten seconds to type their answers and attempt to steal the point. Keep playing until all players have mimed one movie title – and then announce the winning team.

# 5-Minute Monologue

This creative-writing exercise encourages commitment and connection in performance.

Ask all players to source a pen and some paper, and then explain that they are going to write a short monologue with the intriguing title: *Missing*.

This title offers lots of scope for dramatic delivery. It could be told from the perspective of a missing person who is forced by their captor to record a video for their family... or from a family member making an impassioned plea to return their child... or from a kidnapper making demands for the release of a missing person... you get the idea; there are lots of creative possibilities here which make it an ideal choice.

Explain that the monologue doesn't have to be long, but it must be as truthful and emotional as possible. Encourage players not to think too deeply but to feel... and then to write. In such a short amount of time, you are not expecting a work of perfection, but a heartfelt and committed piece. There are no 'wrong' monologues here; this is all about creating. Players should be liberated to set their imaginations free and to write without pressure. Allow five minutes (or ten, if you're feeling kind) to write and let the monologue creation... begin!

When the writing time is up, ask the players in turn to perform their monologues. They should come close to their screens, so the audience can be fully invested in the action and emotion of their work.

The saying goes that 'necessity is the mother of invention', and proof of that is very much in the listening here – the short preparation time will invariably lead to boundless invention and incredible creativity. You will often be amazed by the power of the pieces, and the satisfaction that the players feel at the end of this exercise make it a real favourite.

# 75

# Antiques Roadshow

This fun-filled and creative exercise demands quick thinking and open minds, and asks that players remain cool, calm and collected under pressure.

Ask all the players to source an object from their house or garden. The only brief is that the object should be at least ten years old – other than that, it can be anything at all (as long as it is not a pet or family member!). Once objects have been sourced, insist that players do not reveal them to the group just yet!

Players are about to appear in a one-off antiques show in which they will take turns at being either the antiques expert or the nerve-wracked contestant, anxiously waiting to hear how much their object is worth. Begin by announcing who will be the first expert and which of the players are to reveal their object. Once the object is revealed, the expert has just thirty seconds to give their appraisal and, finally, and perhaps most importantly, to offer their estimate of its value.

The more information that the expert can give about the object, the more compelling the viewing will be: 'It's a small green vase worth ten pounds' will not cut the mustard, but it's far more interesting if the green vase is made out of pure jade, cut from the deepest caves of Narnia, and that this prized possession was once owned by none other than Prince Harry who offered it as a gift to Meghan on their wedding day! You get the idea – the more information the players can provide, the more interesting and intriguing the object will become, and the easier it will be to provide the all-important valuation.

Quick thinking and creativity are vital here. Players should focus on the object and let their imaginations run free, not being afraid to express whatever their minds come up with. Nothing is wrong in this exercise, so players should have the courage just to relax and create. This is so much fun and, the more you play it, the more relaxed the players will become, and the more they will trust in and vocalise their creativity.

# World's Worst

**An improvisation classic, reworked for online compatibility.**

The rules of the game are very simple. First of all, announce a 'World's Worst' category: let's say 'World's Worst Pilot'. With title set, ask the players to put their hand up if they have an idea of what the world's worst pilot might say. Choose one player and hear their contribution:

'You will notice that today's visibility is very low, which is a shame… because I forgot to bring my glasses!'

Now choose another player, who might say:

'Ladies and gentlemen… unfortunately, there will be no drinks service on today's flight because… I just drank them all… hic!'

After a number of players have given their World's Worst Pilot impressions, it's competition time! Divide the players into two teams and decide on another category. Here are some suggestions:

★ Cabin crew.

★ Shop assistant.

★ Kids' TV presenter.

★ Doctor.

★ Swimming instructor.

★ Firefighter.

★ Barber.

★ Acupuncturist.

★ Nanny.

With title decided upon, choose a team to go first; they now have ninety seconds to come up with as many 'World's Worst…' as possible, which they should do by putting their hands up, as before, and making their offer. Count how many successful offers are made and move on to the second team, who then have ninety seconds to come up with as many ideas in their category as they can.

Continue this over three rounds, keeping a tally of the scores until finally awarding one team with the paradoxical title of the 'World's Worst Winners'!

# Topic Tag

**This quick-fire exercise is an effective way of ensuring that all players are actively involved in the session.**

This is a simple exercise, but it works very well in an online setting. First of all, ensure that all players are in 'Gallery View' before announcing the first topic; something relatively simple like:

★ Countries.

★ Modes of transport.

★ Animals you'd find in a zoo.

★ Types of clothing.

★ Musicals.

★ Things you'd find on a beach.

★ Famous singers.

With the category set – let's say 'Things You'd Find on a Beach' – you will start by holding an imaginary ball between two hands, stating a thing you'd find on a beach – 'a deckchair' – before nominating another player – 'Sam' – and throwing the imaginary ball to Sam. Sam must now catch the imaginary ball, say their own beach item – 'a donkey' – before nominating someone else – 'Eliza' – and throwing the ball to her... This continues until all players have had a go at receiving the ball and passing it on.

Once they've got the idea, it's time to add a competitive element to the play by giving a new subject and stating that, this time, there can be no pauses or hesitations before giving an answer. Insist that everyone must receive the ball but no one can receive it twice, and once all players have caught the ball and made their offer, the final player should throw the ball back to you. This is not as easy as you may think, and it's a great way of improving focus and concentration, as the players not only have to think of their suggestion but also remember who has and hasn't received the imaginary ball.

# Channel-Hopping

**This fun-filled exercise calls for concentration, quick thinking and active listening skills.**

Before the session, prepare a number of slips with TV genres written upon them; this kind of thing:

★ Cookery programme.

★ Police drama.

★ Wildlife documentary.

★ The news.

★ Film review.

★ History documentary.

★ Sports report.

★ Charity fundraising show.

Number the players, and then decide what genre they'll be broadcasting by drawing the slips, one at a time, and showing one to each player. With genres decided, it's time to grab your remote control and hop through the channels!

Point your remote at the screen and call a number/channel – 'One!' – and the corresponding player must burst into action and entertain the group with their TV show. After a few seconds, switch to another channel – 'Five!' – at which point, Player 1 must immediately stop broadcasting and Player 5 should burst into life. Keep hopping from channel to channel. When you return to a previously watched channel, the programme should continue from where it left off, until you are content that everyone has had at least one turn.

Now it's knockout time! You are to restart your channel-hopping – only, this time, if players pause, hesitate or start spouting nonsense... turn off their channel and ask the eliminated player to sit away from their screen as you continue hopping. Keep hopping and eliminating until you are left with only one channel: the winner of the Broadcaster of the Year Award!

# 79

# Pass the Potato

**An inclusive exercise that encourages accepting, dramatic escalation and teamwork.**

Number the players, and inform everyone that you have brought a very special item to today's session and that item is... a potato! Now, this is a drama session, so you don't need an actual potato – just use your imagination or, failing that, have every player run to the fridge and grab a real one.

This is no ordinary potato; it's a magical, temperature-changing potato that is used for demonstrating rising action. It will start life as a very cold potato and, as it's passed around the players, it will become increasingly hot until it becomes so unbearably boiling that it's almost impossible to hold!

The cold potato will start its path in the hands of Player 1, so instruct them to hold it out for all to see and to feel the coolness of the refrigerated potato skin against their palms... Now it's time to pass the potato. The potato will be passed from Player 1, to Player 2, to Player 3, and so on, until it returns to Player 1 and the cycle continues! You can do this by calling 'Pass' or, if you prefer, the number of the next player who will receive the potato. On your call, the player in possession of the potato must mime passing the potato and the receiving player must mime receiving it.

Encourage the players to increase the temperature gradually as the potato navigates its way around the group so that it doesn't go from lukewarm to boiling hot in two passes! To ensure success, players must focus on the others within the group (especially the player before them), so that, when they receive the potato, their reaction is a continuation of the work done by their fellow company members and there is a clear, gradual progression in the rising temperature of the spud. If a player noticeably drops the temperature or hikes it up excessively, stop the exercise and start again from the previous player and a cold potato.

Once you've perfected the potato, it's a good idea to try again – but, this time, use a drink which each player mimes sipping before passing on. This is no ordinary drink; it starts off as sweet and thirst-quenching and ends up as the most vomit-inducing, bitter brew ever tasted! Players should convey the changing taste with facial and vocal reactions.

This exercise can only succeed if players demonstrate strong teamwork skills... The more they focus on the others, the more successful they will be, proving that age-old adage: 'It's amazing what lessons can be learnt from passing an imaginary potato.' (Not actually an age-old adage – but use it often and it might become one!)

# How Appealing

This exercise requires players to combine clarity of thinking with persuasiveness and passion.

Announce that, in today's session, all players are on a fundraising mission. They have each been given a twenty-second slot on prime-time TV to make a charity appeal, with the aim of raising as much money as they can for their worthy cause. So, number the players, and inform each player of their cause. The appeals are focused on saving something, but saving what? Well, that's up to you...

★ Save the Whale.

★ Save the Rhino.

★ Save the Double-Stuff Oreo.

★ Save the Sprout.

★ Save the Beard.

★ Save the Ant.

★ Save the TV Talent Show.

As you can see, the causes don't have to be particularly serious! If you are struggling for inspiration, it's always a good idea to ask the players to type in some suggestions in the chat box. From my experience, they will always be alive with ideas, and several of them will be extremely off-the-wall!

With causes decided upon, it's time for the televised appeals to begin. Each player has exactly twenty second to make their appeal, and the more impassioned, convincing and persuasive, the better. The art of persuasion is more important than facts here, so players can make up whatever 'statistics' (i.e. lies!) they like about the last pair of breeding ants in existence or the plight of the world's last beard – the object is to pull on the heartstrings of the watching audience and get the donations flooding in! Other players can type in the chat box how much they'd donate to each cause, though you'll need to have a calculator on hand to tot them up fast.

After all appeals have been made, declare who gave the most persuasive argument and who raised the most money.

# Closing Thoughts

Social distancing must not be seen as an end to creativity. In fact, the current restrictions may prove to be the catalyst for untold invention if we embrace what's possible, rather than lamenting what has been (temporarily) lost. Developing a new way of teaching and leading our students will only serve to broaden all of our horizons, if we have the courage to look towards a whole new world of dramatic possibilities just waiting to be discovered!

The global pandemic has provided an opportunity like never before to rethink the old, and bring a new approach to teaching drama. The more we allow ourselves to embrace these opportunities, the more creativity will emerge during this unprecedented time. So, let's make this period one that will be forever regarded as a time when teaching was reimagined and rediscovered – and our students emerged stimulated, challenged, reinvigorated.

I hope that this book plays its part in reinventing what is possible within the drama session. When we are able to come together again, and the restrictions of social distancing are a distant memory, I trust that drama practitioners and players alike will be better, stronger and more resilient for the experience. By navigating this time with imagination and open minds, when the curtain rises on a new era of live performance, there will be a whole generation of inventive, imaginative, well-rounded and resilient performers primed to take to the stage. At whatever distance, they will be ready once more to bring joy to our lives.

Until that time, stay positive, stay creative and stay safe.

Index
of Games

# Index by Course

*💻 indicates a game suitable for playing online*

## Main Courses

## Desserts

# Index by Game Name

*Numbers refer to game number (rather than page number)*

**www.dramamenu.com**
**www.nickhernbooks.co.uk**

facebook.com/nickhernbooks

twitter.com/nickhernbooks